MEDICINE WOMAN

MEDICINE WOMAN

Lynn V. Andrews

Illustrations by Daniel Reeves

HarperSanFrancisco
A Division of HarperCollins*Publishers*

Lines from Robinson Jeffers' "Tear Life to Pieces" are from *The Beginning and the End and Other Poems: The Last Works of Robinson Jeffers* (New York: Random House, 1963); used by permission.

FIRST HARPERCOLLINS PAPERBACK EDITION PUBLISHED IN 1983

Library of Congress Cataloging in Publication Data

Andrews, Lynn V.
  MEDICINE WOMAN

   1. Cree Indians—Religion and mythology.   2. Indians of North America—Great Plains—Religion and mythology.   3. Andrews, Lynn V. 4. Whistling Elk, Agnes.   I. Title.
E99.D1A53   1981   299'.78   81-47546
ISBN 0-06-250026-0   AACR2

98   **RRD H   40 39**

Acknowledgments

I am deeply grateful to D. H. Latimer, the guiding wolf of many writers. My gratitude and respect for my publisher, Clayton Carlson, speaks for itself. And to Rosalyn Bruyere, a true sister who knows her shadow, my thanks.

A special thanks to my sweet medicine teachers, without whom this book could never have been written.

> There are no medicine men, without medicine women. A medicine man is given power by a woman, and it has always been that way. A medicine man stands in the place of the dog. He is merely an instrument of woman. It doesn't look that way any more, but it is true.
>
> —Agnes Whistling Elk

A yellow moon had risen over the hills in the distance. The sky was beautiful and immense and somewhere the coyotes were singing their mournful song.

I was sitting before an open fire with an old Indian woman. Her face was creased like that of an apple doll. Her cheekbones were high, and her long braids fell well below her shoulders. She wore a beaded medicine wheel necklace over her green plaid Pendleton shirt.

"Your life is a path," she said, her thick accent at first difficult to understand. "Knowingly or unknowingly you have been on a vision quest. It is good to have a vision, a dream."

There was something compelling about her. Her personality seemed to change from moment to moment. Although she had difficulty expressing the simplest thoughts in English, she was as erudite as anyone I have ever known, and she had great dignity.

"Woman is the ultimate," she said. "Mother earth belongs to woman, not man. She carries the void."

These were her words to me before I became her apprentice. She is a heyoka medicine woman. I was destined to follow in her path for seven years. This book is a record of my journey into her strange and beautiful realm—a celebration of the power of woman—as she made me see that power.

I am walking in a part of the faraway. The prairie is covered with sparse scrub-sage and low-spreading cedar. I think of a lonely valley in a crater of the moon. I come upon an ornate cabinet in this strange vast silence. Its craftsmanship is remarkable. I can see through its translucent doors. On its left side, behind the glass, a woman's face is looking at me—the face of an ancient American Indian. On the right side, I see a blue-black crow. The scene reminds me of Magritte painting.

The woman's head begins turning back and forth abruptly—rhythmically, like the beat of a metronome.

"How many times must I tell you," she scolds, still turning back and forth, "the marriage basket is not for sale. You have to earn it. You must earn it."

As I am being chastised, my attention is diverted to the gleaming eye of the crow. The crow's body starts swiveling inward to face the head of the woman, moving in the same metronome-like beat.

I am startled. The crow begins to mimic the speech of the old woman. The two distinct voices are so quarrelsome I shudder.

I've seen only one marriage basket in my life. I happen to know that the basket is still in existence. Where, I don't know.

—Hyemeyohsts Storm

"Are you ready?" asked Ivan, anxious to leave.

"Not just yet," I answered. "Believe it or not, I think I've found something interesting."

I had gone to Grover Gallery for the Stieglitz opening with Dr. Ivan Demetriev, a psychiatrist friend of mine. The gallery was packed with the usual art patrons and pretenders to culture, but I had expected that. That wasn't what bothered me. It was the exhibition. It was static, flavorless.

That was before I saw the photograph.

"Wait a minute, Ivan, that can't be a Stieglitz," I said, tugging at his sleeve. We stood before a photograph of an old American Indian basket. Ivan gave it a grudging look, still bored, still anxious to leave.

"That's a fascinating design," I said, looking closer, "but not at all like Stieglitz." I kept peering at the basket, which was haunting. It had an intricate pattern resembling a dolphin with a snake, or with lightning. Even though I am a collector of American Indian art, I had never seen anything to compare with it. There was something unusual about the weave as well. I couldn't tell whether it was coiled or woven, or what. I was entranced by its perfection. No telling where it was from, but it was already on display in my subconscious. Ivan kept frowning and looking to the exits. The print, an 8 x 10, had a mystic sepia quality that I would never have associated with Stieglitz. I wondered at what stage he had done it. My eyes fell on the neatly typed paper legend below the picture, and I looked for the date. It was there all right, along with the title, "The Marriage Basket," but I was in for another surprise. The photographer's name was listed as McKinnley. It was a lone island in a sea of Stieglitzes.

Ivan was looking at me impatiently.

"Are you familiar with the photographer, McKinnley?" I asked.

"No, I don't recognize him," he said, pulling my arm. "But I recognize a bunch of phonies and pseudo-intellectuals when I see them, so let's get out of here and get a drink."

"But I want that photograph," I said.

"Come back tomorrow and get it on your own time," Ivan said, brusquely heading for the door.

"At least let me write down the name," I said rustling around unsuccessfully in my purse for a pen. I looked up, saw Ivan waving me outside, and with a sigh decided I could remember "Marriage Basket" and "McKinnley." I ran to catch up with Ivan.

That night the strange dreams began. I couldn't sleep. An owl hooted ominously in the walnut tree outside my bedroom. I pulled the covers up around my face, and lay rigid and silent. As I began to drift towards sleep, images of the marriage basket, dark and mysterious, centered in my night vision. The dream imploded into a wild whirring sound in my consciousness. I awoke with a start and sat upright in bed, wide-eyed, frightened. Then I threw off the covers angrily and stomped into the bathroom. I flicked the light on and rummaged noisily around in the medicine cabinet, glancing suspiciously at the mirrors for any sign of flitting shadows. An aspirin bottle slipped to the floor and broke into a dozen pieces. As I bent to sweep up the pills and glass I banged my head. "Damn."

I took a swig of Alka-Seltzer and lurched back to bed. The room was dark except for wands of moonlight that played on my face. I thought of an Anaïs Nin story in which the heroine basked in the light of the moon, turned and trembled under that awesome glow, and slowly lost her soul. As I dropped off to sleep the owl hooted and the marriage basket loomed in front of me again, this time held out in a foreboding gesture by an old Indian woman with eyes like polished mirrors. The vision kept reappearing until I passed out from exhaustion.

The next thing I knew the phone rang. It was morning.

"Hello," I said, not fully awake.

"Lynn Andrews, please. Grover Gallery returning her call," said a maddeningly cheerful female voice.

"Yes, this is me, she. I left a message with your answering service last night regarding a photograph of a marriage basket that I saw during the Stieglitz exhibition. Will you please hold it for me?"

"A marriage basket, ma'am?"

"Yes, an American Indian marriage basket photographed by McKinnley, I believe. I'm not even sure. I think it was McKinnley."

"McKinnley?"

"Yes, no. An old picture by some photographer."

"Let me check, Ms. Andrews." She put me on hold and the phone was disconnected. The dial tone buzzed.

I hung up and held my aching head. A few moments later the phone rang again.

"Ms. Andrews?"

"Yes."

"We have no such photograph listed by McKinnley or any other photographer."

"What do you mean you don't have the photograph?" I sat bolt upright, suddenly alert.

"There is no record of our having an American Indian marriage basket, Ms. Andrews." Her voice was impatient.

"But that's impossible. I mean, there must be an error. I'll be right down, thank you."

I was strangely obsessed, almost frantic. I wove through traffic to the gallery on La Cienega Boulevard, physically exhausted from the previous night, addled with confusion over the morning phone call, and scornful of their lack of efficiency in simple record keeping. I parked in front and stalked into the gallery. The vast expanse of white walls, the collision of photographs hanging at eye level in every direction, revolted me—as did, at that moment, the entire "in" art scene. The "in" art dealer approached me, scanning my Jaguar sedan outside and my old Gucci bag. The man was sharp-featured, wiry, and pretentious.

"Ms. Andrews?"

"Yes. I called about the photograph of the marriage basket. I saw it here last night. It was by McKinnley." My voice was strained and unfamiliar.

"Let me interrupt you, ma'am. First of all, please sit down and let's have a cup of tea. Do you take cream or sugar? Fine." He left the room without waiting for my answer.

I sat down on the only piece of furniture in the gallery, a round, overstuffed, donut-shaped sofa with a raised upholstered pedestal in the middle. It was covered in orange fake fur and designed so that there was no possible way to be comfortable. The man returned with two cups of tea and handed me one as he sat down. We sat back-to-back in aggravated silence, sipping tea. I decided to let him speak first. With growing paranoia, I was becoming convinced that he was hiding the photograph from me so that I would pay more for it.

"Ms. Andrews, there must be some mistake. We have searched through our records, and we have only one McKinnley photograph." He paused and turned to look at me, craning his neck stiffly, catching himself from falling off the orange donut.

"Well, let me see that photograph, please."

He shrugged, eyes cast up to the white ceiling, and left the room again. He was gone for an interminable period of time, and I was sure he was preparing to set an astronomical figure on the print. I sat twirling the fake orange fur into little balls with my nervous fingers, staring at the photographs on the walls. Ominous masks stared back at me, black and white echos of my recent nightmares. I stood up and started to pace. He returned with a small portfolio, glared at me, and said with an incongruously sweet tone, "Here you are, Ms. Andrews." He opened the portfolio on the orange seat to an old sepia picture of tipis on the Little Big Horn, circa 1850. I grabbed the picture, searching under it furiously for the photograph of the marriage basket. The portfolio was empty.

"You're lying," I said.

The little man jumped back and hastily exclaimed, "I told you that we do not have the photograph, and to my knowledge we never did. Really, Ms. Andrews, I think this is getting a little out of hand."

Realizing my imprudence, my ill temper and total lack of control, I excused myself and fled from the gallery. I careened down La Cienega and back to Beverly Hills. Arriving home, I made another cup of tea and sank into the sofa, my cold feet propped up. Then I reached for the telephone and dialed Ivan's number.

"Dr. Demetriev's office," the secretary answered. "May I help you?"

"Please may I speak to Ivan. This is Lynn Andrews."

"The doctor is with a patient. Give me your number and I'll have him return your call."

"This is urgent. Please tell him I'm on the line."

She put me on hold. Muzak insulted my ears.

"Hello," Ivan said brusquely.

"Ivan, remember that marriage basket last night. What was the name of the photographer?"

"What marriage basket? What photograph? I'm in the middle of a suicidal breakdown, so make it quick, Lynn."

"I'm sorry to interrupt, but I have to know about that particular photograph last night at the gallery. Don't you remember?"

"I don't remember any photograph of any basket," he said with finality. "And it was a Stieglitz exhibition. I don't appreciate this kind of interruption."

"But I showed it to you just as we were leaving."

5

"Lynn, I think you better check with my secretary and make an appointment," he teased. "You didn't show me any photograph of any basket, I assure you."

"Ivan, are you absolutely certain? This is important. It was an old sepia print, at least seventy years old—by McKinnley, I think."

"I'm positive that you showed me no such photograph. I'll call you later." He hung up.

My head was spinning. I knew I had seen that damned photograph. I had touched it with my hands and seen it in my dream. What was going on? Suddenly I felt very tired.

I looked around my living room. It was like sitting in the center of a combination African village and American Indian museum. Over the years I had relentlessly gathered a priceless collection of Congolese ancestral figures, magical fetishes and war gods, Navajo blankets, and baskets from all over North America and Guatemala. The room was magical, full of the poetry and power of ancient primitive traditions. The baskets, symmetrical and perfect, that lined the walls were my favorites. And that marriage basket, imbued with magic—never had I felt so compelled to acquire an object.

I settled back in my chair, trying to get comfortable, and looked across the room at an earlier obsession, a black and white hand-woven fertility sash from Guatemala. It hung down the wall next to a photograph of the Grand Jaguar Mayan Temple I had taken in Tikal, Guatemala, a couple of months ago. I recalled the difficulties of the month-long search for the sash.

I had driven in a rented jeep from Guatemala City toward Chichicastenego—an ancient Indian market place where, it was said, I would find the particular sash I was determined to have. The countryside was breathtaking—patchwork farmland and a sophisticated network of irrigation ditches terraced the sides of the hills—irrigation had been practiced by the Mayan Guatemalans for centuries. The land was fertile and green. I could smell the rich earth and the smoke from wood fires in the thatch-roofed houses. I reached the ascent to Chi Chi with the sun high overhead. The ancient village was situated on top of a high mesa and the road was treacherous, even with the jeep's four-wheel drive.

About halfway up the narrow switchbacks, the traffic in both directions was halted and I had to stop. An enormous circus truck carrying a mother elephant and her baby had swung wide, trying to round a curve, and nearly gone off the cliff. Evidently the road had been blocked for hours.

I turned off the ignition and got out onto the roadside. Hosts of excited birds chattered in the great cathedral of trees that touched high overhead. The reverse gear in the circus truck was gone, and with every movement of the two elephants the truck creaked and groaned. One car after another pulled up. Angry Guatemalans shouted insults and advice to the flustered driver.

The commotion heightened. The elephant and her baby kept swaying the truck back and forth, and the old boards of its wooden side panels started to crack. It rocked precariously, two feet from the edge of a thousand-foot drop. Absolute bedlam ensued. Just then a long bus filled with circus performers pulled up.

Deformed midgets with rusty chains on their backs, fat ladies and tattooed baldheaded men with levers and pulleys poured out of the bus. Tightrope walkers and acrobats and belly dancers, all Guatemalan, short and brown, hollered for the tourists to get the hell out of the way.

The elephants trumpeted screams of terror, the truck swayed threateningly close to the abyss and to certain death for the animals. The midgets were crawling around under the truck shouting obscenities. Fifty or so people watched the spectacle— bermuda-clad tourists, Guatemalans, Indians in traditional long dresses and *huipiles* balancing market-ready baskets on their heads. We were breathless.

One of the midgets drew a chain around the axle of the truck and someone else attached the chain to the bumper of the bus. The truck driver put his engine into neutral gear and the bus engine was started. It was hard to believe that the bumper held, let alone the old rusty chain. As the truck began to move backward, the fat lady and the tattooed man removed the rocks from behind the tires, flinging them aside as if they were pebbles. Now, with the new movement, the elephants stopped swaying. The midgets jumped up and down and turned somersaults in midair and the entire forest resounded with cheers from us all. The circus went on its way.

I continued to Chi Chi only to be told that I had to fly to a remote province of Guatemala, to the ancient Mayan ruins of Tikal-Peten, to find a trader who might sell me the sash. Back to the jeep and Guatemala City, a half day's drive away.

What a flight to Tikal-Peten! There were ten seats, and I was the only passenger. The plane was an old army transport, World War II vintage. I could see the jungles of Guatemala between the floor boards. We were scheduled to arrive at the small airport at 6:00 A.M., but even that early in the morning it was oppressively hot and damp. The pilot circled the fifty square miles of partially exposed ruins jutting awesomely out of the vast expanse of dense jungle, waiting until a local farmer pulled a cow out of the way to put down on the dirt landing strip.

The museum located at the airstrip for the benefit of the tourists was nearly deserted. The woman there told me that the trader I was looking for had gone back to Guatemala City, gave me an address, and said that the next plane left in four hours. I was disappointed.

I bought a can of cold juice and a map, and learned from a guide how to walk to the main court of the Grand Jaguar Temple. I loaded my camera with film before starting up the hard-packed path. The din of the jungle birds taunted me, and the early morning air was heavily perfumed with allspice. The path was flanked with giant palms, and fern-like trees flowered brilliantly with cymbidium vines. Soaking wet with the ever rising heat, I tied my white shirt above my waist. I was utterly alone amid the massive stone aqueducts, platforms, and stellas, and I was so intensely fascinated with the hieroglyphs and stone carvings, so heady with the opiate of perfume in the air, that I didn't realize I was altogether lost.

I turned a blind corner into a small open courtyard and bumped against a tall Indian man. I yelled in surprise.

"What are you doing here?" he asked. His face was young and beautiful, and he stood quite still. "You should be in the north."

"Do you mean in the city?" I asked.

He looked at me sternly and continued talking as if he knew me. "You must revisit the city, but your journey is to the far north."

"How do I get back to the airstrip?" I asked nervously, wanting to end this conversation.

"Sit down," he said.

He smoothed the ground between us and, using a stick, carefully etched a map in the dirt, and pointed in the direction I should go. He took great care to help me understand him, and I noticed his remarkable grace and elegance as he spoke. When he finished, I felt I should give him something for his trouble and rummaged through my shoulder bag, but the only thing I could find was money—a twenty dollar bill. As he took it, a strange light flashed in his eyes and he looked at me intently.

"This money that you have given me binds you," he said. "I will send you two helpers within forty-four days. The first helper will be female. You will not recognize her as your ally. This ally you must conquer. I will also send you a male helper, who will mark your trail." He ripped the twenty dollar bill in half and gave half back to me, saying, "Keep this."

I was startled and irked.

"We will meet again," he said. "Keep this broken money in your bundle."

"Do you mean my purse?"

But our conversation was finished, and he only pointed forcefully with the stick and said, "Don't ever come back to this place. Hurry."

I had no wish to offend the man, who was obviously insane. I could return to Guatemala and the temples any time I wanted to. I indicated that I understood.

"Hurry from here or you will never find your way."

He stood up and walked off, disappearing almost instantly into the jungle. My first impulse was to throw the worthless scrap of money away, but I stuffed it behind a credit card in my wallet. I headed for the airstrip, Guatemala City, and the coveted fertility sash.

Now the sash hung on my wall. It was beautiful, certainly worth the effort it had taken to find. I took another sip of tea, realizing with a start that it had been more than a month since that experience with the young Indian. Well, so much for him, I thought. There certainly was no female helper in view, whatever he meant by that.

"If I have to stay here tonight I'll go mad," I said out loud. I leaned forward and picked up a silver box that stood on my coffee table, opened the top, and took out a piece of paper with a scribbled name and date on it. My old friend Arthur Desser was giving a dinner party on February 18th at eight—that very evening. I stuffed the invitation back inside the box. My nerves were frayed because of the gallery incident and lack of sleep. I began to wonder if I'd imagined the marriage basket photograph. I even flipped through last weekend's Calendar section of the *Times* to check for the Stieglitz exhibition. The show was advertised.

Then I lost control again. I even made several futile phone calls to galleries in New York. No one had a McKinnley photograph of a marriage basket, although one had—possibly—heard of one. I needed a dose of reality. I decided to go to Elizabeth Arden's and have a pedicure.

When I got back home, I sat on the edge of my bed for a while, rubbing my newly painted toes over the soft deerskin rug. Then, setting the alarm two hours ahead, I buried my head in my pillow and fell asleep.

"No, no, no," I heard my voice screaming in the distance. Suddenly, I was awake. I was flailing around, covered with perspiration, pillows everywhere as though I had flung them about. I sat up, still seeing the dream, and pushed away the air in front of me, as though there were a giant burden on my chest. The vision *couldn't* have been simply a dream. I had seen her so clearly, a little girl with uncanny shining eyes, holding the marriage basket towards me. She had been beckoning me to come closer, closer, closer, and then suddenly she began to grow tall and the basket became enormous. She rushed towards me, menacing me with the outstretched basket.

"Oh my God, not again," I said. I flipped on the light, holding my satin comforter around me, and glanced at the clock. Just then the alarm went off, and I pressed the "off button" and lay back shivering on the few remaining pillows. I wanted to get up and turn on every light in the house.

I was shaking as I got out of bed and dressed for Arthur's party. I drove over to Bel Air, not ten minutes away, along Carolwood Drive past Walt Disney's home. I remembered Leon Craig, the developer of Bel Air, who lived on an estate next to Disney's that included a Versailles-like expanse of garden with many acres of neatly tended paths and hedges and endless rose gardens stretching serene and perfect around the rambling house. Papa, as his family called him, a charming and endearing man who lived all alone in that enormous home except for occasional visits from his family, was an alcoholic, a man who had everything in the world yet drank himself into oblivion. I used to wonder about him. Papa was like many friends of my parents, the first half of their lives bent on the struggle to amass a fortune, the last years spent in a malaise of bitterness and self-destruction. I didn't want my life to end like that.

The symbols of wealth stretched away on either side of the winding road. I slowed my car to look at the exquisite gardens, their trees forming long and stately corridors, the leaves shining in the moonlight. Those manicured shrubs and flower beds, weeded and lined up as if with a compass, were a great comfort to me, the ordered, opulent universe of Bel Air was familiar. Usually I would drink in the air and the quiet and wonder why a person would want to live anywhere else. Yet tonight I felt like a discharged battery. I drove faster, my eyes back on the road.

Three miles farther on I came to Arthur's. I could see lights in the windows and hear music. There were about ten cars parked on the street—Rolls Royces, Mercedeses, a mammoth four-wheel drive pickup with a camper on top. I wondered who Arthur had gathered together this time. Arthur delights in intellectual soirees, pitting scientist and entrepreneur against artist and guru. Arthur, who made his sizeable fortune in the oil refining business, is four times divorced with two children, and has been on nearly every psychic and psychological trip there is. It has got him nowhere, and though I love Arthur, I am wary of him. You never know what he will do—particularly at this kind of dinner party.

A tin voice came over the buzz box, with an accent. It was the French maid.

"Françoise, it's Lynn Andrews here."

There was a clicking noise and Françoise opened the massive laquered Chinese gates.

"Comment ça va?" I asked.

"Très bien, merci, Mademoiselle Andrews. C'est magnifique!" she exclaimed, pulling at my black silk crepe kimono and patting me on the arm affectionately. Suddenly from around the green tiled pool came the "Hounds of Baskerville," as I call Arthur's Yorkshire Terriers, small, shaggy pillows of rage, snarling and barking.

"Oh be careful of that one, Mademoiselle Andrews," Françoise said in alarm. "Remember, he bites."

"Merlin won't bite me. He knows me."

Merlin growled at me; sniffed my toes and blithely sank his sharp little teeth into my silken pants leg.

"Ouch, you little devil . . . !" I yelled, kicking him off me. He hadn't broken the skin, but there were a few tooth holes in my pants.

"Naughty dog!" Françoise scolded.

She bent forward and shooed the three dogs into the kennel room, still yipping and growling.

I started up the brick stairs to the living room. There were votive candles on each step, bright pink flowers trailing down from the balcony above. Arthur stood smiling at the top of the stairs, dressed in his traditional Yale blue blazer and gray flannel slacks, a cocktail in his hand.

"Darling, you're late," he said.

"Your dog just bit me, little monster!"

"He has a tendency to do that. Come in, darling. I love your hair. I have some very important people for you to meet."

He took my kimono and put it in the closet.

"What exactly are you up to tonight, Arthur?"

"Well, I have a special surprise for you, an American Indian medicine man who wrote that best-selling book *Seven Arrows*. Have you heard of him?"

"Yes. I'm delighted."

"I thought you would be," Arthur said sarcastically. We walked into the rectangular white living room. A fire was crackling in the fireplace. Ray Howlett's reflective light-box art threw subtle prisms of pastel over the vaulted ceiling. A Fritz Scholder painting covered the entire wall behind the long leather sofa, and a serene Buddha, six feet tall and crumbling with age, held court over us all.

Arthur introduced his guests. "Lynn, I would like you to meet my oldest and dearest friends from Connecticut, George Helmstead and his wife Pamela. George is in banking."

"Hello," I said.

"You know Ivan Demetriev."

We hugged each other.

"And my girlfriend, Helen, who is celebrating a big insurance deal tonight."

"That's great," I said, eyeing her with curiosity.

"Have you met Dr. Friedlander and Lorraine?"

"I don't believe so."

"Dr. Friedlander is studying anti-aging. He has just returned from India."

"I'm happy to meet you." I shook hands with the doctor. His head was shaven, turning pink and blue in the glow of Howlett's light-box. His Fu Manchu moustache was appropriate, and his eyes twinkled. Lorraine was tall, with a panther-like beauty. She smiled at me.

Arthur then introduced me to an actress who had been my

favorite for years. She wore balloon pants and a feather boa.

"Now, last but not least, may I present Hyemeyohsts Storm, author of *Seven Arrows*." I extended my hand in greeting. My first impression of him was of a stillness vast as the North. Arthur brought me a vodka and tonic, and I barely noticed taking the drink. Storm and I began to talk about his book, and about Jumping Mouse, my favorite part. As we talked I knew something was taking hold of me. Many people dream of finding a reflection within themselves of a person, no matter how ordinary, who will somehow bring beauty into their lives. I felt something like that, and it wasn't anything Storm said or did. Maybe it was just his presence, or his friendship. To this day, I don't know. But I was aware of being grounded, of suddenly stepping into a magic circle with Storm—so that I was at once behind him and around him. External things that had been comforting and familiar moments before now became sources of discomfort and restriction, and I was uneasy.

The maid broke into our reverie, announcing dinner, and everyone got up, drinks in hand. We snaked across the balcony garden in the cold night air and wound down the spiral chrome staircase into the Valley of the Thankas—my name for Arthur's dining room, because it was lined with Tibetan art. I noticed that Arthur and Helen were weaving a bit. That meant the rest of the evening would get heavy.

"What do you think?" Arthur whispered, indicating Storm.

"Very interesting," I said simply. Arthur seated us around a long wooden table with a beautiful flower arrangement in the center. The crystal and silver sparkled. Arthur sat at the head of the table and placed Storm at the other end, in the "hot seat." I sat to the right of Storm. Françoise and another French maid began to serve us wilted spinach salad and pour one of two wines served. Everyone was talking about the anti-aging research Dr. Friedlander was doing.

"Frankly, I think I'll just have a zipper installed up my back," said the actress.

The tone was easy and pleasant as we finished our salads.

"This evening I hope you will feel free to say anything or do anything that you want to do," Arthur interjected.

"All right, Arthur, but let's say it with humor and not irony this evening," joked Ivan in his attractive Russian accent.

"No limitations, no limitations," said Helen, raising her glass to toast her own words. Françoise began to serve the main dish of squab and wild rice.

"Never assume limitation. You will only suffer the death of it," the actress said, cutting open the breast of the squab to reveal the stuffing. "Don't you agree, Ivan?"

"Yes. While alive you will probably feel as though you were dying; you will feel lost." He leered at her.

"I think that the only answer to the search in this world is Freudian analysis," Arthur said, after pouring more wine.

"The only answer is to do what you want, and if you aren't able to, find someone else to do it for you," said the banker from Connecticut.

Arthur turned to me. "Lynn, I think anyone who aligns himself with the American Indian is a loser." Françoise was taking away the dinner dishes, the other maid serving crème caramel.

"Do you think I'm a loser?" I asked, used to his onslaughts.

"As far as Indians are concerned, yes. And what do you think of that, Mr. Storm?"

"Not much," Storm said quietly. "Incidentally, the only way I'll talk with you, Mr. Desser, is as an equal."

The room was quiet.

"Just what do you mean?" asked Arthur.

"I'll demonstrate to you," said Storm. His presence was affecting everyone around him. "Say 'Ivan doesn't matter.'" This man seemed mysterious and deep as a canyon. He was definitely Dakota or Montana. You could feel it.

"Ivan doesn't matter," mimicked Arthur.

"Say 'Lynn doesn't matter.'"

"Lynn doesn't matter."

"Say 'Helen doesn't matter.' " After going through all the guests and coming to himself, Storm said, "If you're not willing to do that, then I won't talk with you."

"You don't matter and I still think you're a loser," Arthur said vehemently. He refilled his glass.

"Okay, I don't care if you want to play with me. I'll play with you," Storm said in a decidedly ominous tone.

I redirected the conversation by asking Dr. Friedlander what he had been doing in India.

"I was conducting research, though my method will sound odd and unscientific at best. I'm interested in the ability of some people to lower their body temperature at will. We've found that if a body is kept at a lower temperature, the aging process is retarded. I've been meditating for years, and I've known yogis who could maintain a trancelike state for days, resulting, I hoped, in a lower body temperature. I went to India in search of yogis to test."

"And how did you check their temperature?" asked the actress.

"Well, this may sound funny, but I used a rectal thermometer. I went around India sticking thermometers up yogis' asses."

Everyone roared with laughter except Arthur, who had been whispering angrily in Helen's ear. Suddenly he ordered her to leave the room and she ran from the table in tears.

Ignoring the fight, I asked, "Did you find that the yogis maintained a lower temperature?"

"Only in a few instances did I find a marked difference."

"Did you run into any really heavy gurus on your travels?" asked Ivan.

"There were a few. The masters no one has ever heard of in the mountains, they were powerful. There was one who stripped me nude and had me carrying rock to build him a temple. This was in the middle of the jungle. There were months when I did all of the work for him and his students. He finally let me take his temperature, and then he made me tear down everything I'd built."

Arthur interrupted. "Mr. Storm, in your world wouldn't you be considered a kind of yogi?"

"Yes, I am."

"Then why doesn't Dr. Friedlander stick a thermometer up your ass?" Arthur looked rabid.

Everyone gasped in surprise.

Storm got up quietly and walked around the table, his eyes holding Arthur's, the space between the two men electric with tension. Storm reached down in front of Arthur's stomach. His hand seemed to disappear into the solar plexus, then turned and twisted as if he were pulling out intestines. Arthur jerked heavily.

"I did that for you, Lynn," Storm said, looking directly at me. "I took his will. Now we can talk."

Storm returned to his seat. The other guests seemed unaware of what had just happened and talked in a ritualistic party way as did Arthur, who no longer seemed drunk. They seemed hypnotized, and when Storm and I began to speak no one seemed to hear us. But we didn't speak of what had just taken place—I was afraid to. Finally, I asked him in a shaky voice if he had ever heard of a marriage basket.

"I have seen one marriage basket in my life," he said, ignoring the entranced guests around him.

"You have?" I asked excitedly, almost forgetting what had just occurred.

"I happen to know that the basket is still in existence. Where, I don't know."

"But you must know where I can find it," I persisted.

He studied me impassively, then said very carefully, "If I wanted to find the keeper of the basket I would go to the Cree Reserve north of Crowley, Manitoba." He hesitated, taking a long drag from his cigarette and watching me intently, and went on. "I would try to find an old woman named Agnes Whistling Elk. She is a heyoka, as they call some medicine women—a woman-who-shows-how. No one knows exactly where Agnes lives. She moves around quite a lot and seems to prefer it that way."

"How can I find her if I don't have her address?"

"Agnes is very difficult to nail down. Luckily, there is another woman who can help you if she wants to, Ruby Plenty Chiefs. I'm sure Ruby will know where to locate Agnes, but I can't promise she will help you. Ruby is also very secretive—set in her ways. You may go all the way to Manitoba only for Ruby to tell you to turn around and go home. No amount of persuasion can make her move if she doesn't want to."

"Is there any certain way I should approach this Ruby Plenty Chiefs?"

"Yes, bring her tobacco, a carton of cigarettes, and an Indian trade blanket. That is the custom. Remember that the marriage basket is sacred. Don't delude yourself into supposing you can have it just because you want it. You can have the basket only if you're worthy."

"Crowley in Manitoba?" I asked weakly, thinking, Here I go again.

"Why do you want this particular basket? There are many beautiful Indian baskets that are much less dangerous." Somehow I knew he was playing with me.

"I saw a photograph of a marriage basket at the Stieglitz exhibition the other night. Ever since, I have had dreams about it. I am obsessed by this basket. I must find it or at least a picture of it. The photograph I saw was not at the gallery the next day and they had no record of it. In fact, this has been a nightmare."

"Are you a collector of artifacts?" he asked.

"I am a collector and dealer in North American Indian art and, in particular, baskets."

"You are going to have to go to a lot of trouble to find the marriage basket. It is a very sacred and high symbol in the world of dreamers."

"Dreamers?"

"Yes, dreamers."

"What is a dreamer?"

"The dreamers are those who see the dream of themselves and others, but this is not the time to discuss it. If you are serious I will draw you a map showing the way to the Cree Reserve from the Winnipeg Airport. Here is my phone number."

He wrote his number on a piece of paper, hastily drew a crude map on the back of it, and pressed the paper into my hand. Then he smiled warmly at me, said good night to the group, and left. Only then did I realize he had put a small piece of gray fur in my hand as well. Everyone was still behaving very strangely, and we all went home shortly thereafter.

The next morning Arthur woke me with a phone call. "Lynn, was I too awful last night?"

"Arthur, you have to stop drinking."

"I'm sorry. I'm embarrassed."

"The food was fabulous."

"I don't know what I did last night but I have a terrible bruise around my stomach and solar plexus. It hurts like hell."

"Arthur, thanks again for the party. I'll ring you later after I get up. Maybe you took a fall."

What is the voice of woman but the voice of the katchina?
—Agnes Whistling Elk

My Air Canada 727 landed at the Winnipeg Airport and I rented a car. In thirty minutes I was speeding down the highway toward Crowley, following Storm's map. I opened the car window and took a first deep breath of crisp Canadian air. What in the world was I doing, out in the Canadian tundra meeting an old woman about a basket?

Driving, a vision of the basket swept through my mind, and for a moment there was a contrast of light and darkness and a vast space opening up before me. Then the road focused again, tedious and deserted, and I blinked to clear my head. I gripped the wheel more firmly.

I wondered if I had the right clothing. I was wearing Sasson jeans, boots, and a khaki hunting jacket from Kerr's. My valise was stuffed with sweaters, wool socks, flannel pajamas, and my makeup bag. I felt slightly cold and turned on the heater. The radio worked, but the reception was poor and I clicked it off.

The sky was enormous, and in every direction I could see the great airy landscape of Manitoba. Across the grand rolling fields the green grasses twisted and curled in the wind.

Suddenly the hood of my car pitched down to the left. My left front tire had blown out. "Damn it!" I yelled, furiously hanging on to the wheel as the car fishtailed across the road onto the soft shoulder on the other side. I skidded to a halt, no longer

21

daydreaming about Canada's pastoral beauty. I sat a moment catching my breath and then jerked open the door. "Just my luck."

I got out angrily, kicked at the mutilated tire, and stomped around looking for a sign of life, help, a phone. There was nothing of the sort in view. I realized I had not seen a car since the outskirts of Winnipeg. Well, since there was no AAA around, I would have to change the tire myself. I dragged the tire equipment to the front of the car, breaking my fingernail in the process, and sat down in the dirt to figure out how to use the jack. At least there was one, but it took me half an hour to figure out how to place the thing under the frame.

As I was leaning forward on my knees to insert the lever, I caught sight of two silhouetted figures, tall, thin, walking down the highway toward me. I jumped up to wave and yell, then caught myself. They were two young Indian men, and I became a little frightened. As they drew nearer I could hear them talking together in a language I presumed was Cree. One of them was wearing a brown plaid mackinaw, the other a tattered army field jacket. They came up to the car, and the one in the mackinaw bent to look at the tire. Then he rose up, and he and the other man broke out laughing. They stared at me with toothy grins and spoke together in Cree. I was angry now.

"Is there a phone anywhere near?"

The grins widened.

"Do you speak English?" (Many reservation Indians don't.)

The man in the mackinaw shrugged his shoulders. Neither made a move to help me.

"Thanks a lot, you creeps."

I went back on my knees to wrestle with the jack. Thirty minutes later, I was covered with grease and tire black, sweating and exhausted, but the tire was changed. I hoped it wasn't going to fall off as I was driving.

I couldn't believe the Indians had simply stood there and watched. I threw the jack and lug wrench into the trunk and stood looking at them. They were standing ten feet away, still staring.

"You're a couple of real jerks."

I was about to get in the car and speed off when the man in the tattered field jacket began to wring his hands as if he were washing them. I thought it was an odd thing to do but gave it no particular significance. He shrugged his shoulders, threw back his head, and began gesturing in some kind of sign language. I felt a considerable tension under my chin and inside my throat, and I wondered if there was a connection between what he was doing with his hands and what was happening to me. My eyes blurred for a few seconds, and when they focused the man was standing very erect, his hands at his sides. Both of them watched me sharply.

"Would you like a ride?" I asked suddenly, surprised at myself.

The man in the tattered jacket smiled. "Sure, we'd love one. Thank you, ma'am." I was amazed to hear him speak perfect English. They crawled into the back of the car and we drove away. The tire seemed okay.

Filled with anger, I decided to ignore the two men. The ribbon of asphalt road stretched ahead for what appeared to be endless miles. I was starving. We drove in silence, the trees like statues in the distance. I began to feel more at one with the lonely expanse of rolling prairie.

The Indian in the tattered field jacket began to chant softly. "He ya he ya hey hey ooaaaah." His friend joined him.

I looked at them in the rearview mirror. They chanted with their eyes closed, nodding their heads with each beat. My eyes back on the road, I slowed for a rabbit.

"He ya he yah oooooah I'm a lonesome cowboy he ya he yah oooooah."

I was startled by the interpolation. In the rearview mirror, the Indian in the mackinaw was still chanting. His eyes met mine, and I blushed.

Suddenly a bird with an enormous wingspan loomed up directly ahead. I swerved, but the bird swooped above us and glided easily out of sight. The Indians instantly chanted very loudly, then abruptly quit.

"We will get out now."

I looked around the landscape for a house or even a path.

Nothing, only the wild expanse of prairie. I pulled over and stopped.

"Are you sure you want to get out here?"

"Yes," said the man in the mackinaw, not looking at me as he opened the door on the passenger side and let in a sudden blast of cool air. I hadn't remembered a wind.

"Enjoy your drive," the man in the army jacket said. With a sharp backward glance, he walked away with his friend. They quickly disappeared over a low hill.

Back on the highway, I noticed giant shadows of merging clouds ghost-walking slowly across the prairie floor. I watched the bluish puffs rolling and reforming and rolling again, their edges sharp and electric. The shadows kept hiding things from me—teasing me. I would watch a stand of poplar trees off in the distance disappear, then reappear as the hills unfolded. There was no sign of human life and I was in a hurry to get to Crowley, but I drove for what seemed hours before I finally got there. The lines on the map indicated a dead end.

There were five or six buildings. Over the door of one a sign read: COUNTRY STORE AND TRADING POST/CROWLEY. An Indian woman and two children came out, slamming a screen door behind them. I parked my car between a battered pickup pulling a loaded horse-trailer and a newer one full of brown, round-faced children eating Hostess cupcakes. The kids looked at me and giggled, and shoved chocolate and crumbs into their mouths. I got out of the car as another pickup truck pulling a horse-trailer was arriving in a cloud of dust. An Indian dressed cowboy-style got out. He was heavyset—two hundred pounds or more.

"Hey lady, you here for the rodeo?" he asked.

"No, I didn't know there was one."

"Well, now you know," he said, smiling. "We'll be roping down the road 'till dark."

"Thank you but I'm looking for a friend." The less involvement other than business the better, as far as I was concerned.

"Yeah, who might that be?" he asked, taking a swig from a beer can.

"I'm looking for a woman named Ruby Plenty Chiefs." Swirling dust from the road blew into my eyes, and I sneezed and wiped at them.

"Never heard of her. You sure you got the right reserve?" He looked at me oddly. "See ya," he said, tipping his Stetson, and went inside the store. I followed, first stamping my feet.

The store was piled high with canned foods, spare tires, motor oil, cupcakes, fan belts, and magazines. A jumble of papers tacked to a bulletin board fluttered noisily from the ever opening and closing door. An ice cream cooler filled with milk and assorted colas stood in the back. Fritos and potato chips hung from high racks to the floor. A pair of brown eyes in the center of this chaos was checking me out coldly.

"Do you want some help?" the owner asked loudly. I jumped. "No."

I perused the store quickly, and resignedly took three packages of Twinkies off the rack.

The roper said, "This lady is looking for someone named Ruby Plenty Chiefs."

The owner showed no sign of recognition. The few Indians in the store who had been studying my every move, averted their eyes. I fumbled around in my purse for money as the owner silently waited on three children and the roper. He stared straight at me.

"She used to live down the road past the Indian Museum, or I guess she was up on Black Mesa." He went on counting out change to the roper.

"Don't you know where she is now?" I asked.

The owner turned to a man in the back of the store. "Hey Emmet, do you know where Ruby lives?"

"Yeah," he called. "She used to live down the road but she moved a year ago."

The roper shrugged his shoulders. "Come to the rodeo instead."

"Some other time," I mumbled.

He shrugged again and left, slamming the screen door. Dust billowed inside.

"Please," I said. "Hyemeyohsts Storm said that I could ask anyone in Crowley where Ruby Plenty Chiefs lives and they'd tell me."

The man cracked a smile and spit tobacco juice on the floor. "You might try going down the gumble—that's what we call the blacktop around here—five and three-quarter miles. Take a left on the dirt road after the bridge and go about four miles. You can't miss the cabin. It's on the right. Listen, are you considering paying for these Twinkies?"

I paid and walked out quickly, the screen door banging shut in a gust of wind. I got into the car, feeling dirt on my hands as I took hold of the wheel. After I checked my gas tank and made a mental note of the mileage, I started down the road towards Ruby Plenty Chiefs' cabin, eating a Twinkie.

I went five and three-quarter miles exactly and caught sight of a dirt road winding off to the left over a hill. Its surface was heavily rutted and I bounced and skidded along at fifteen miles an hour. The wind had died down, and my windshield was collecting so much dust that I had to stop and wipe it twice. Then I saw a cabin between rocks and trees about half a mile ahead, but no sign of life except for a red-tailed hawk circling above.

When I could make out the simple, square log cabin, I slowed the car almost to a stop. There was a huge brown motionless animal on the porch which, as the car crept closer, I realized was two deer. I stopped. Just as I opened the car door and got out an old Indian woman carrying an enormous butcher knife came out of the front door and stood there, glaring her welcome. I was frozen to the spot with fear.

The woman was wearing a long wool skirt and a wool mackinaw—red and black. Her long gray hair was pulled back in a single braid, her face brown and etched with lines. She rolled up her sleeves, still holding the knife menacingly in front of her.

"Are you Ruby Plenty Chiefs?" I stammered.

"Yes," she said, making a move toward me with the now outstretched knife, still looking angry at the intrusion.

"Hyemeyohsts Storm sent me. He said that you could help me

find Agnes Whistling Elk." I had backed up to my car for a fast getaway, and I was almost yelling.

"Yes," she said, "I know that."

I felt absurd. I could imagine how I appeared—a mad blond mess covered with grease and dust and crumbs.

"May I come in and have a cup of tea?" I asked. I took a step toward the porch.

Ruby nodded, turned, and went inside. I assumed I was meant to follow, but stopped on the porch to eye the dead deer. Just then Ruby came back out and stood directly in front of me, this time with another butcher knife in the other hand. Her unusual ancient eyes held the light of a young child—an impatient one. She thrust the butcher knife toward me and commanded me to help her cut up the deer.

"We will talk of your journey later," she said. "And we will speak of the marriage basket." She grabbed my arm with the strength of a man and said, "Quickly, let's get to work."

I was horrified. She handed me the butcher knife and said harshly, "Do what I do, quickly, before the stiffening sets in."

The two deer were lying on their sides. She knelt down, moved them into a better position, and turned to me, jabbing her knife to indicate that I should get on with it. This woman was the key to my finding the basket, so I knelt and began. Ruby was cutting around the hind hooves, so I raised the knife and drew the blade along the edge of the hoof. At the sight of the blood and the scritching sound of the flesh splitting, tears began rolling down my face. I continued, trying to imitate Ruby, first not cutting deep enough, then losing patience and angrily thrusting the knife through the bone—one senseless hack and the hoof separated onto the porch. I wanted to scream.

The old woman took her time now, slicing under the skin on the inside of each leg all the way to the belly. She seemed to take a maniacal glee in the butchering, and she made sure that I was following along. I did my best, until all the skin on each leg was peeled back. When Ruby turned her deer on its side, I managed to wrestle mine over as well. I was splattered with blood, my hands and knife sticky. Suddenly Ruby disemboweled her deer, so fast that the mass of entrails and gore burst out on the porch before I could prepare myself for the sight of it. I stabbed, probed, with my eyes closed. Then I looked down in the intestines. There was a fetus, and milk running from the mother's teats. I felt wave after wave of nausea. I backed away and closed my eyes, unaware of the cabin and the silent process of time, my confusion increased by the sudden darkness.

I don't know how much time elapsed, but when I opened my eyes I was standing with the maimed and fragmented carcasses, and Ruby was nowhere to be seen.

She came out of the cabin, spread newspaper on the porch floor between the animals, and went at her deer again, this time cutting out liver, kidney, and heart. She tossed the liver and kidney, one at a time, on top of the newspaper, and held the still-warm heart in her hands.

"Good," she said, blood dripping from her fingers. "You do it."

I gasped in terror.

"Do it."

I managed to extract each of the organs. My jacket and jeans were saturated with blood. As I cut out the heart, Ruby stood, turned to the east, and lifted her deer's heart to the deepening sky. She began singing in Cree. Her song filled my heart, and I looked up at the now brilliant moon and the bare spring sky. Ruby slowly turned toward me, still singing, a lustre in her eyes. "Hey eeeeh hey yeeh." The song stopped, there was a deliberate silence, and then she said, "That is called lightning song. It is sung to comfort the spirit of the deer."

Ruby sliced off a piece of the deer's heart, began to eat it, and indicated with her knife for me to do the same.

"Oh no," I moaned.

I jabbed the blade into the heart and put a small piece of the warm, tough meat into my mouth. I chewed and gagged, my mouth full of blood.

"Ho," she said, nodding approval.

We began our work again. We cut away the skin, rolling it up into a bundle. The wide eyes of the deer gleamed in the moonlight. By now I was beyond any sense of caring.

Following Ruby's lead, I removed the head. I cut the flank and tenderloin, throwing each piece into a cardboard box. We filled four boxes with blood-soaked meat, and Ruby threw the guts to several dogs that had come snooping around. They leapt on it growling and tearing, and ran away snarling, trailing long strings of intestines.

I was relieved when the butchering was over, and so exhausted and numb that all I wanted to do was sleep. Ruby carried a box of the fresh meat indoors, then returned for another. I wondered when she was going to invite me inside, but she carried all the boxes in and did not return. Timidly, I knocked on her door with my blood-caked fist.

She opened it. "What?"

"I have to wash my hands. May I come in? I need a place to sleep."

"Wash in the morning." She slammed the door in my face.

"Wait a minute," I called. "Where am I going to sleep?"

I heard her say harshly, "Go sleep in your car, wasichu."

My God, she didn't expect me to do that. She couldn't. I looked around for a water hose.

I stared at her door for several minutes as it slowly dawned on me that I was going to have to sleep in my car, then trudged back and tried to make myself as comfortable as I could in the back seat. I heard the cry of some wild animal and locked all the doors. I didn't get much sleep.

I woke up in the morning with Ruby rapping on the window. The old woman was holding a tin can and two large pieces of dried deer flesh—"jerky." I opened the door and took it, too sleepy to do anything more than nod my appreciation. The can was filled with a bitter liquid that smelled like coffee.

After the food I went up to the cabin. I noticed that the head of the deer had been partially eaten. The hooves and other parts were gone, and the blood had been washed, or lapped, off the porch floor. Ruby came out carrying a hatchet, headed for a stack of dead wood by the side of the cabin, and hacked away, ignoring me.

I remembered the trade blanket and tobacco in the trunk of my car. I got them, walked over to Ruby, and handed them to her. "Ruby, I came here from a long way away. I realize I'm an intruder and not very welcome."

Ruby kept chopping.

"Please accept this blanket and tobacco. I need your help. I told you I'm trying to find the marriage basket. Do you know where Agnes Whistling Elk lives?"

"Yes, I know," she said, cracking a branch over her knee. Taking the blanket and cigarettes, and setting them on the woodpile, Ruby turned slowly to look at me. "She lives nine miles from here. Her trail is due east." She took out one of the cigarettes and lit it. "There is no way to get there except to walk. But I wouldn't do that if I were you until I had befriended my dogs."

"Your dogs?"

"Yes, the reserve animals are very fierce, nearly wild. They have killed more than one man and even some children. Most of the time they are away hunting. They join together in packs and run for miles. I know they have killed many deer, and sometimes they turn on their own kind. Nothing can stand up to them. You must introduce yourself, and they must know you, before you go trudging off around here. The dogs are more dangerous than you can imagine."

"What do I have to do? Do I just pet them or what?"

"I will call them, and you must stand perfectly still. Show no fear or it may be the end. I don't believe I could stop them if you made a wrong move and they charged you."

"Can something really happen to me?"

Ruby didn't answer. Instead, she whistled shrilly, and thirty or so dogs came bounding from every direction, every size, shape, and color, and milled around us. They saw that there was no food to be had, and a great black ugly creature growled and barked. Then all the dogs began to yap and bark, snarl and drool. Ruby carried an arm load of wood inside. "Wait," I tried to whisper.

I knew that if any one of the dogs set off a chain reaction, I would be ripped apart. I had to push fear into the recesses of my mind. They drew slowly nearer, sniffing and panting, growing bolder. I checked an impulse to scream. Several cold noses poked underneath my cuffs and up my legs, more than one nose paying particular interest to my crotch. The great black dog leapt up on me with its forepaws and licked my face, another threatened my back, still another chewed on my boot. I stifled the impulse to run.

Ruby came out on the porch and watched, but did nothing.

"Get the hell out of here," she finally yelled. The dogs scampered off in a fright.

"They know you well enough now."

Tears stung my eyes, and my knees buckled. Now that the ordeal was over, my whole body shook.

"Those dogs won't bother you—you can be glad of that," Ruby said, her eyes laughing strangely. "You can go about this country as you please. Not knowing the dogs, you were taking a big gamble. You have a chance to get to Agnes' house now; before you didn't."

My hands were clasped tightly, and I realized I was cutting off circulation. "Yes," I said.

"Go your way now, wasichu. Maybe you'll find what you're looking for. Here." She handed me three pieces of dried meat and I took them. She walked away laughing. "The marriage basket. The wasichu don't know anything."

I stood there foolishly, holding the meat, then walked to my car and got a few things for my trek to Agnes'.

I started out from Ruby's house on the trail. Nine miles was really not very far, and I had my parka tied around my waist and an extra sweater in my shoulder bag.

The dew was still on the grass. I walked around the rocks behind Ruby's cabin following the path, a wide peaceful valley before me. The grass was green, and the few trees were blooming with spring. A stream meandered next to the trail. I did a few stretching exercises for the kinks in my back, and tried to erase the dogs from my mind. Then I started jogging up the trail, slowly, and got almost to the end of the valley, two or three miles. I walked for a while, crows flying overhead, and stopped near a pool where the stream widened, at a large flat rock warm from the sun. I lay down on it, ate a piece of jerky, and grew drowsy watching the white puffs of clouds above. Squirrels were playing in a nearby tree, their chatter underscoring the awesome silence. I took a deep breath, grateful for real air. I could feel the freshness of it on my tongue.

I lay on my stomach and poked my finger into the reflection of my face in the pool. Tiny waves rippled outwards from the center. I had no idea why I was following this obsession. The vague sensation—a mixture of fear and expectation—was still there, as it had been since I first saw the photograph. I knew that I was going into unfamiliar territory. I looked down at the warm, inviting water.

"Why not?" I needed a bath.

I took off my clothes and slipped into the clear water, and sat submerged up to my neck on a mossy underwater ledge. Half dreaming, I watched the patterns reflected on the surface from the light above.

I don't know how long I floated there, but a cold gust of wind woke me quickly. The gathering black clouds had blotted out the sun. When I tried to stand up, my foot slipped on the moss. I grabbed for the rock ledge behind me, realized that I was dizzy and disoriented, and floundered in the water, which had turned black, reflecting the sky. I found a foothold and started to crawl out of the water, slipped again, and lurched forward with a splash, hitting my face on the rock. My nose started to bleed. I scrambled out—so dizzy I could hardly find my clothes. My head began to clear, and I tried to wipe the blood off my white sweater. It left a long red stain. I could hear thunder in the distance, and it was getting darker. I started to run slowly, saving my strength—what was left of it. The trail led over a low hill and then up over a mesa. The going was rough.

It thundered overhead. I could see giant black faces in the clouds. I was conscious of every breath as if someone else were breathing me. I felt I was being watched. Finally, I saw them. The magpies that had been flying around were perched in a tree up ahead—facing the trail. Dull black eyes followed as I ran by. They were eerie and aggressive. But I struggled ahead toward a wide canyon. Rain was sheeting down in the slate gray distance. A cold wind blew down the rock cliffs to the north, and I zipped my parka up around my neck and jogged on. Then the trail narrowed and disappeared. Dejected, I sat down in the dirt and held my head in my hands.

My heart was pounding, my mouth dry. A crow flew overhead cawing. I was scared out of my wits, but there was something inside me pulling me toward my dream. I got up to orient myself. I looked down through the canyon, high mesa cliffs on either side and an open end. A creek ran down the center, and I decided that if I were a trail I would follow it. I was angry now—Ruby had known that the trail ended nowhere. She had told me, however, to walk due east, and the canyon stretched east ahead of me. I started off across the grassy floor.

I ran the length of the canyon, rain still threatening, hills forlorn and desolate in their mantle of gray. Then, almost without realizing it, my feet felt a worn path beneath them. Thank God. It started to sprinkle and I ran on, nearing total exhaustion, my sense of time gone. I seemed to be standing still, but I knew I had gone well over eight miles.

The rain began in earnest just as I approached a stand of cottonwood trees and large rocks. I stopped dead. I saw the form of a cabin blurred into the mesa. Did it belong to Agnes Whistling Elk? I didn't care, I was so tired and wet and frightened. There was no sign of life, no animal or person. I picked up a big stick in one hand and a rock in the other, just in case there were dogs like Ruby had said, and approached. I climbed the rickety porch and knocked on the door—no answer. I knocked again in desperation, and this time the door opened. No one was inside. A bed stood in the corner, covered with an Indian blanket. It appeared to be a Two Grey Hills design, and I caught myself wondering if I could buy it and if this was Agnes' cabin.

Kerosene lamps stood on the window sill. A blue enameled wash basin sat on a rough wood counter next to the wood-burning stove. Bunches of herbs hung from nails in the log walls. Pieces of cardboard were nailed up here and there for insulation—even a tin Coca-Cola sign was used. At the foot of the bed was a crude dresser with a Mexican black velvet painting of a Spanish dancer above it. Next to that hung several deer-foot rattles and an owl wing. I noticed two apples on the gray wooden table in the center of the room. There were three chairs.

I sat down and voraciously ate an apple. The rain pounded on the tin above my head. I had never been alone in the wilderness in my life. I closed the front door—the room was freezing. The night shadows were lengthening, edging the courage out of me. I stomped around to hear myself, and talked to myself as I lit the kerosene lamp and tried, with no success, to light the wood stove. My body had completely given out. I ate some jerky from the wall and, in freezing desperation, took the old sleeping bag I saw in the corner and spread it out on the bed. It was stained with oil, and had a blue-and-pink Mickey Mouse flannel lining. I had taken off my soaked clothes and started to crawl in before I realized I badly needed to pee.

Groaning, I put my parka and boots back on and tentatively opened the front door. A lightning flash lit up the porch, and I saw it was empty. I crept outside and down the stairs, and squatted on the wet grass in the torrents of rain, holding on to the porch for security. Then I hurriedly went back inside and closed the door, now really wet. I undressed again, crawled quickly into bed, shivering and shaking, and turned out the kerosene lamp. The rain had stopped, and now it was too silent. I lay rigid in bed.

I don't know how long I slept but suddenly I was shaken awake. Someone was pulling my hair, gouging my shoulder, and shouting at me.

"Get up! It's time. Get up quickly!"

I opened my eyes and gasped. In the flickering candlelight I saw a face that looked like melted wax. I wasn't sure if the face was human. I screamed, and a hand closed over my mouth.

"It's time!"

I turned my face away, unable to regain my equilibrium. "What's the matter?" I asked. "Are you Agnes Whistling Elk?"

"Yes, you're in my cabin. Get up and follow me—right now!"

I scrambled up and threw on my jeans, parka, and boots. Agnes shoved me with surprising strength toward the door. I almost fell.

"What in the hell are you doing?"

Agnes shoved me harder. "We have to hurry."

I was so stiff I could hardly walk, but we headed away from the cabin in the moonlight at a dead run, the old woman moving like a young girl, and into the rocks behind the cabin. There was no path. We crawled up over boulders and around jutting cliffs that made enormous ghostlike shadows. I slipped and fell, twisting my ankle and bruising my knee, but Agnes grabbed my hand and yanked me forward. We must have kept up this crazy pace for over fifteen minutes.

We reached a clearing in the rocks. Not twenty yards away stood a luminous tipi. The exterior glowed from the firelight within, and smoke curled from the top. It was surreal. Agnes dragged me to the entrance.

"Naked!" she demanded.

"What?"

"You must face the grandparents naked."

With incredible speed, Agnes turned and ripped every stitch of clothing off my body. I tried to protest, but she slapped me. My ears were ringing, and I was shaking with fear. My senses were reeling as Agnes pushed me into the lodge ahead of her.

Six old Indian women wrapped in blankets were sitting around a central fire. A heavy pungent smoke hung in the air. In the red-tinged glow I could see that their faces were older even than Agnes'. Behind them, ribbons hung from the lodge poles—and feathers and gourds and buffalo skulls. There were prayer sticks stuck in the mounds of earth in front of four of the women.

"Sit down," Agnes said, pushing me to the ground.

She moved to my right and sat down next to me. I shivered, holding my knees to cover my breasts.

Eyes glittered at me collectively, and the shadows thrown by the firelight danced around the tipi walls. Thoughts of medieval witches' covens raced through my head. Treasured images of beautiful ancient Indian women out of photographs by Curtis seemed to be in front of me. But now they were mocking—glaring at me viciously.

"Why did you bring this cannibal now, Agnes?" one of the old women said in broken English. Her voice was mean. I must have jumped visibly at the word *cannibal*.

The woman sitting nearest to me was holding a long staff or walking stick with feathers hanging from it. She began poking, first my shoulder and then my side, with the point. Another woman bent forward and pinched me.

"This child wants to walk the road of the marriage basket," said Agnes.

I didn't dare move under this horrible probing.

"Ho," said the woman with the staff. "Why have you been so long in coming here?" When I turned to face her, a chill ran through me.

"I only came to buy the marriage basket if it's the same one I saw in the picture—if it doesn't cost too much." I was babbling.

"Quiet, idiot," Agnes said.

"But I just wanted the basket to . . . "

"Quiet!" Agnes hissed. "Speak only when you're spoken to."

"She's not ready," the woman with the staff said. She leaned over and whispered to Agnes.

The other old women nodded their heads. I felt victim to some terrible conspiracy.

"You can never teach her," someone said.

Then I heard a sound I could only describe as cackling, something like birds or madness. The old women all began to scold me at once—it was too much. I knew I was about to go insane.

"Please, I just want to see the marriage basket." I didn't recognize the sound of my own voice.

The woman with the staff eyed me coldly. "We will pray for

you. We will dream for you," she said. I didn't understand.

I felt vertigo, the ground went out from under me, and I fell backward. The faces of the old women seemed to be younger, their eyes like mirrors. I saw the girl in my nightmare. A deer was sitting in the place of the nearest old woman, and there were other beasts—a wolf, a lynx, and certain animals I did not recognize. The lodge whirled into a blur and I passed out.

I woke up late the next morning to the smell of the wood-burning stove. Could this still be part of the dream? For a moment I didn't know where I was. Agnes was steeping tea.

"Eat," Agnes said. "Breakfast is ready."

I got up, put on my clothes, and went to the table. Agnes brought two tin pie-plates and put them at our places. She sat down across from me. I was trembling and very hungry. Outside the cabin window, a pale light was reflected in the trees. It was raining. I looked down at the food—deer jerky, blackberries, fried bread, and sage tea—and abandoned myself to eating. Everything was wonderful.

"What happened last night? Did I pass out? How did I get back here?" I asked Agnes, now that I was comfortable.

"Just eat," she said, motioning at my plate. She left the table and sat on the bed I had been sleeping on. I noticed her picking up my torn jacket.

I let the steam from the sage tea warm my face. The small cardboard box of jerky on the table had dried blood all over the sides. I didn't care, it was wonderful. I kept on eating ravenously.

Agnes was sewing a tear in my jacket. With all my will and courage, I asked, "Are you going to sell me the marriage basket?"

"You don't know, Lynn, but you are in a very dangerous circumstance." Agnes kept working the needle, but glanced up and smiled. It was the first time she had used my name.

"What does the basket mean, and why am I so obsessed with finding the damn thing anyway?"

Agnes seemed sweet and gentle. "You don't understand." She bit the thread and knotted it, and put the mended jacket to one side. "If you do not listen to the womanness within yourself you are going to perish. Perhaps you will have the marriage basket one day, perhaps not. But it is your choice. You will have to make the decision. No one can make it for you, not even the grandparents."

Her words didn't make any sense whatsoever, but her tone was disarming. Agnes was so different from the ogre I had experienced last night I wondered if she was the same person. Her slap still smarted on my cheek. I knew I should hate her for humiliating me, but I didn't. The food was a comfort, and the sound of the rain pelting on the tin roof was soothing.

"What do you mean, it's my decision? What in the world are you talking about? I'm an art collector."

"You don't know what you are," she said. "There is no explaining why you are born, or why you are the animated part of the earth you are. You think that I don't know you or anything about you. But I can tell you an experience that you had. I've never seen the great lakes of this world, the ocean. But I can tell you that one day the water washed over you. So the womb of this world has chosen you and given you protection. That was a power sign to you, a gift from the womb of your mother, the earth, and that is why the dreamers have reached you. There is no explaining why you have been chosen. All that is left for you is the knowing."

I knew the event she was referring to instantly. One afternoon in Venice, California, I walked down on the beach, climbed up on the rocks, and stood there watching the turquoise green of the sea. For no apparent reason, the water suddenly lifted at least thirty feet in the air and covered me, only me and no one else near me. I hung on the rocks, thoroughly drenched and laughing, until the lifeguards came with bullhorns telling everyone to get off the jetty.

Agnes poured more sage tea. We sat in the silence for several minutes, my thoughts in turmoil. "The basket is the ancient way of woman," she said very softly.

For some reason I started to cry, then babble. "Those mean old women—especially Ruby Plenty Chiefs. She made me cut up that deer. The way she came at me with her knife, I thought she was going to stab me or hack me to pieces. It was horrible. Nothing like this has ever happened to me. It's unfair. I hate that old hag."

"There's no need to hate her," Agnes said, stopping me. "She wasn't trying to hurt you. Ruby is blind."

"Blind!" I said, still crying. "No. She can't be blind. I don't believe it. Oh, I'm so sorry."

"Never apologize," Agnes said sternly. "I'll speak of Ruby if you like but you must listen carefully. Her story has meaning for you."

"You'd just never know she's blind—tell me." I wiped my eyes.

"When Ruby was sixteen she was going to marry Stuart Runs Backward. He was a good man but that was a long time ago. He's dead now. She lived with her grandfather. One day when he was out trapping and Ruby was staying at home, she heard a loud racket. That was in the days before cars, when everyone had wagons or rode on horseback. The racket got very loud, and she looked out the window and saw a horseless iron wagon with smoke coming out of the front. Four government land surveyors stood beside it arguing.

"One came to the cabin and beat on the door. Ruby was afraid. She hadn't seen too many white people before. They were dressed funny, and two were wearing pistols. The man at the door kept yelling. Finally, he pounded so hard that the leather hinge snapped and the door fell in. He saw Ruby standing by the window, and I think he was very startled to see this beautiful young girl. Maybe he thought that an old deaf man lived there in that cabin. He came over and grabbed her by the arm and said some awful-sounding words. Ruby didn't understand them, but they made her feel ashamed.

"The three other men came up to see who was in there with the first man and went inside the cabin. Ruby realized she was in real trouble. She knew those wasichu were going to rape her, and she tried to break the window and run away. Someone struck her and shoved her in the corner. One of those men was a big man. He took off his belt, put it around her neck, and pulled her by it to the bed. They ripped off her clothes. Ruby pleaded with them but they didn't hear her. She started to scream and fight, and managed to pull away from the belt and grab a piece of firewood. There was a hell of a battle—I think those four men were really surprised.

They got angry and beat her but they weren't satisfied, so they all took turns and raped her.

"Then they wondered if they should kill her. Many people said that Ruby would have been better off dead than what became of her. One of the men wanted to give her money so she wouldn't say anything about being raped. They knew they wouldn't get in much trouble for what they'd done because she was an Indian, but it would cost their white families embarrassment. They didn't have the stomach to kill her, so they took a compass they used to make their maps with. It had a sharp point on it. They wanted to make sure she couldn't identify them. So before they left, they made sure she was blind.

"When Ruby's grandfather came back home and saw what had happened, he fed her broth and gathered herbs to heal her. She got her strength back pretty soon, but all she did was sit around the cabin, soiling herself and refusing to learn or care for herself. She even asked her grandfather to kill her, but he hit her and said he would not tolerate her self-indulgence. He said she had been given a unique enemy—her blindness. Ruby said she didn't care—she wanted to be dead. Her beauty had been spoiled, and her chance for a happy life. She was lucky, though, because her grandfather was a medicine man and not so very old. He had been learning a long time and had great power.

"He could see that her will was sleeping and that he had to wake up her stomach. He began by acting very nice, but he tricked her many times. He made her trip and fall down, handed her scalding hot utensils, and put things on her plate that couldn't be eaten. He teased her and aroused her anger until he could see that her stomach was coming alive. Ruby was hurt. She felt that her grandfather no longer loved her.

"All during that time he sat outside in the moonlight, singing many songs asking for guidance so that Ruby could be completed. By and by one night he saw a mother raccoon and her children. This was a sign to send her north, the sign he had been waiting for. She went.

"Those Sautoux up there didn't know anything about white

people. Their power wasn't taken away. Their power was not hidden. Those were big medicine people, and their dances were still magic. As I said, that was a long time ago.

"There was a medicine man named Four Deer who even those Sautoux were afraid of. He went to live on the high mountain, where he could see down to his village from his lean-to. They said that Four Deer had the power to bring back life even from dead people, that he took his power from women who did not see him. Even I do not understand this medicine. All those Sautoux made Ruby climb the mountain, but no one would go with her. They were too afraid of Four Deer. She fell down many times and bruised and scratched herself. Four Deer was watching her, not saying anything, but somehow she felt him and was drawn up the mountain to him. When she got up there Four Deer was laughing. Ruby asked what she must do. He said he only had one way to help her. She would always be blind, but he could make her complete if he killed her and worked his medicine within her death. Then he would take this power of the women who did not see him and restore her life. After that she must learn from the Sautoux women about deer medicine. She must eat a broth made from deer feet and eat only deer meat from then on. Otherwise she would die.

"Four Deer built a platform and laid her on it, took a pipe stem, and blew some poison into her ears. Ruby died, and her spirit went away to the the campground of the newly dead. Four Deer did his medicine, refashioned something in her body, and called upon the power of the women who could not see him to bring her spirit back. This took many days. Then he put something that Ruby told me was very cold in her mouth and she woke up, sicker than she had ever been. She went into a strange seizure. Four Deer made her use the energy generated by the seizure to feel in all directions. He taught her through control of this energy.

"Now Ruby is blind but she sees more than anyone. Four Deer led her to the center of this outwardly violent circle and taught her how to quiet herself. She will always see because she is always in that center. He told her to go first to the Sautoux women, then to go back to her grandfather and let his songs teach her. Ruby is a medicine woman. She knows more about deer medicine than anyone. Four Deer and those Sautoux women taught her everything. I hope she gives away her medicine, because there are many who need it.

"I'm not telling you about Ruby to amuse you. I'm telling you to instruct you," Agnes went on. "I'm a medicine woman. I live in the beyond and come back, and you went there with me last night. You are being initiated into a knowledge as old as time. The dreamers have touched you. Sometimes you can look back over your shoulder and not pay any attention. You can choose to be blind, or you can follow your destiny."

Agnes' face was patient. It slowly began to dawn on me that I was being drawn by a force beyond my understanding. I started to piece together the events of the last months. I sat back in my chair, heavy, paralyzed. The thought occurred to me that this wasn't a situation of possession, but that in being chosen I too chose. With each revulsion, each terror, I became more fixated on my dream of the basket. It wasn't clear what held me, whether it was the seeker within me or the nightmare, but what did it matter?

Agnes must have sensed my surrender, for she smiled and nodded her head. Without a word she started to clean off the table. I stared at the weathered wood and the crumbs from the fried bread. My life was in those crumbs, and I knew it but didn't care.

Agnes touched my shoulder and said, "Come, you're going back to California."

"How can I go back?" I asked. "I don't have the basket. I can't go home yet."

Agnes put on a heavy wool shirt and sternly handed me my parka.

"We're going to Ruby's," she said. "I'm sending you home."

She went over to her dresser, picked up something, and put it on the table in front of me. It was an antler-tip earring inlaid with turquoise.

"Ruby told me if you happened to show up to give this earring to you. Take it—it is protection."

"Protection? What do I need protection from? How can an earring protect me?"

"Put it on," she ordered. "Let no man ever touch it except a heyoka man in his woman time."

I put the earring on. Agnes was going out the door, and I grabbed my bag and followed her.

"A woman is born pregnant," Agnes said, as we walked along side by side. "A man has to be impregnated by woman. Some men achieve this through plants or other disciplines. There are secrets I can't yet tell you."

We walked west on the trail as Agnes spoke. "There are different kinds of forces in the world. These powers can kill you easily or make you wish you were dead. When you decide to obtain the marriage basket against all the forces that have ever been, you will need courage and will. The earring will help you in the crossing from your world to mine."

Agnes motioned for me to walk faster. I had trouble keeping up with her without running.

"The things that have helped you in the past in your world—your credit cards, your car, the clothes you wear—those things are not practical here and will not help you."

The air was clear, the good smell of damp earth welcome. We walked a mile or so in the silence. The thought of that illuminated tipi in the night kept bothering me, that and the word "cannibal" the old woman had used.

I finally asked, "Last night, Agnes, what did they mean, 'cannibal'?"

Agnes smiled. Still walking, she took a thin piece of jerky out of the breast pocket of her wool shirt and shoved it toward my mouth, indicating that I should eat. I took a bite though I wasn't hungry and it was hard to chew.

We came to the place where the trail ended and started down into the canyon. Flowers were blooming after the rain. The colors were vibrant, the blooms moving in the soft wind.

"Last night you visited the grandparents," she said. "They are giving away to me because you have been chosen by the dreamers.

The grandparents are helping me to teach you. You have come into what for you is a strange world. There is much you don't understand."

Agnes stopped abruptly. She squatted down in a patch of flowers and lifted up the face of a blue flower. I leaned over to look at it.

"When you can talk to a plant," she said, "when you know that a plant is alive, has a spirit, you eat the plant and the plant gives away to you. You have the power from the spirit of the plant." She picked up the flower and ate it. "I'm looking at you and I see that you don't understand what I'm saying."

Nervously, I took a bite of deer jerky.

"The meat that you are eating now, that is your sister. We eat our brothers and sisters. You're a cannibal. Your sister has fallen down so that you may have life."

I nodded understanding, and we started again. The canyon was full of birds, prairie dogs, and butterflies, all busy with spring.

"Yes," I said. "I think I understand a little bit about why you think of people as cannibals. But I don't understand why I had to be so humiliated. I mean, you stripped me naked in front of all those old women—the grandparents," I corrected myself.

"To begin to take your first awkward steps on the red road of womanhood you must be naked in every way," Agnes said.

We went around the edge of the canyon and saw the stream and pool in the distance. I looked at the outcropping of rocks and saw once again how beautiful the pool was.

Agnes suddenly asked, a change in her mood, "Are you a woman?"

"Yes."

"Are you a woman when you are naked?"

"Yes," I answered.

"Do you have a vagina?"

"Yes."

I couldn't imagine what she meant by this line of questioning.

"Do you menstruate?"

"Yes."

"We didn't know. In the native world it is called your moon. It is your time of greatest power. Last night we had to make sure."

I blushed. We walked the rest of the way to the flat rock by the water in silence. I was happy to rest. We ate more jerky and drank from the stream. I lay back on the rock contented and sleepy, shut my eyes, and yawned.

Suddenly there was a loud explosive sound like the crack of a rifle.

"Wake up!" Agnes yelled at me. I jumped up and spun around.

"How do you know I won't kill you?" she asked, dropping two large rocks on the ground, one from each hand. She was menacing. She looked larger than before.

"Sit," she said, pointing to the ground. "Now we will speak of the marriage basket. You should know something so you'll know what you're up against.

"A man came out here one time—just a man. His name was Father Pearson. He said he knew everything about two kinds of looking. He could look up and see and hear the good spirits. Down somewhere in the mother earth were the bad spirits. He held up the sign of the crossed trails and said that we were not balanced. He said if we didn't start looking up, the good spirits would kill us. Everybody in those days thought this was pretty funny.

"Old man Twin Coyotes felt sorry for him and decided to teach him. He showed him what was in everybody's medicine bundle, but every time Twin Coyotes started teaching him about women, the priest got very angry. Twin Coyotes told him if he truly wanted to learn the use of power he would have to go and learn from me. He didn't like that, but he was intelligent and he listened. There are no medicine men, without medicine women. A medicine man is given power by a woman, and it has always been that way. A medicine man stands in the place of the dog. He is merely an instrument of woman. It doesn't look that way anymore, but it is true.

"He came to me and, since Twin Coyotes was my friend, I took him as my initiate. He was cunning and learned fast. I knew he was falling in love with me as he progressed in my instruction—it is that way often with men. I didn't love this white man or even like him. But I saw he was becoming powerful.

"One day he confessed his love to me and wanted to possess me. He wanted my power, but I didn't want to give it to him. I told him that he would have to find another woman of ability. Jealousy was virtually unknown among my people at that time, but I saw his eyes turn to hate. Hate is a power I understand, and I decided to make him live with the taste of it in his mouth. Hate tastes like burnt corn. When it advances with wisdom, there's almost no stopping the power of it.

"I made him wear a mask from that time till the end of my instruction. There are masks you can make that can hold emotions—every heyoka knows that. It's a simple thing to take a stitch in your face with a bone needle and you can go around happy and full of love—that is also a mask. But the mask that this man wore was one to contain hate.

"He learned as much as any man can learn. He knows the native world as well as anyone, and he can do anything he wants. You won't understand this, but he is made out of power. I showed him all about being a medicine man, but he wasn't interested in that. He took the knowledge and became a powerful sorcerer instead. Little by little he learned it all, and now he is as strong as any magician on earth. He threw down his vestments, got a name, and learned how to be hidden. His name is The-Man-Who-Picks-Up-The-Trail, or Disguised Trail. Some say his name is Fire Dog or Fire Soldier. We who know him call him Red Dog.

"I used to be the keeper of the marriage basket. It was woven from the dreams of many women, produced and renewed by the efforts of the weavers and the dreamers. It is very beautiful, and sacred to all women. This Red Dog found the basket one day when I was meeting with Twin Coyotes. I didn't expect him to steal it, but he did. He had to get himself something he could use as his giveaway power woman, so he stole the basket. It had more power than any single woman.

"I can't give you the basket. You have to steal it back from Red

46

Dog, and I can't think of anything more dangerous. I am willing to teach you how to steal it because he cannot hurt me. But he can kill you easily, and he is always alert. It won't be easy to steal, but if you are brave you might be able to do it. I cannot steal it back myself, because that is the law of the dreamers. I hope you are willing."

"Steal! I couldn't steal anything," I said righteously.

Agnes fixed me with an evil stare.

"I've never stolen anything in my life," I lied.

"I'm interested in your ability, not your morals. If you want the basket you have to learn to steal."

No one is a sorcerer every hour of the day. How could you live?
—Pablo Picasso

Holmby Park was deserted at seven in the morning except for a few joggers and a couple of elderly gentlemen walking their dogs on leashes. I touched my toes, took some deep breaths, and started to run slowly down the path leading to the bowling greens. The grass was damp and fragrant, the water from the sprinklers like crystals. I looked up at the trees and affluent estates surrounding the park. The last time I had run was in Canada. No tree-lined boulevards there—just the vast expanse of the Canadian steppes.

Agnes had instructed me to contemplate returning to Canada very carefully. I would be there for several weeks, perhaps months, and perhaps I would never be able to leave Agnes. Perhaps I would die there. She would teach me to steal the marriage basket if I chose to become a person in the position of learning. But here in Los Angeles I was erecting every obstacle imaginable—terror, laziness, mainly my eternal doubt. I kept thinking that there was no rush, always time. I rounded the south end of the park. It was good to resume my jogging routine.

By the time I got back to my house I was dripping wet and exhausted. After showering I wrapped myself in a terrycloth robe and combed my hair out, my thoughts full of baskets and ugly old women.

I walked to the bedroom and put on a white dress and high heels. I wanted to keep moving, to escape my thoughts. I drove distractedly to the Bistro Garden to meet my girlfriend Caroline.

"Well, you look in a great mood," Caroline said. There had always been a devil-may-care quality to our friendship. Seeing Caroline was reassuring.

"I'm in a state," I said.

"Well?"

"I may be off to Canada in a day or two to go live with that medicine woman I told you about. We'll see. That's all I can tell you. I'm just going crazy, that's all."

"You've done some strange things, but going to Canada to live with head hunters or whoever they are, that's a bit much."

I stared blankly at Caroline and took a sip of my martini. The drink burned my lips, but it felt just right—poisonous and good. I was instantly drunk.

The Bistro was crowded with elegant people. Etched glass partitions and polished brass divided the rows of tables, each set with a dazzling bouquet of flowers. The mirrored walls reflected endless lines of beautiful smiling faces, all normal but totally absurd. I forced myself to sit erect and still on the red upholstered bench.

Our poached salmon arrived. I poured bernaise sauce from a silver pitcher, remembering the cardboard box covered with blood.

"What's the matter with you?" Caroline asked.

"Caroline, wouldn't you like to come up to Canada with me?" I asked jokingly. "It isn't Rio, but we could stay at this quaint little cabin I know about. The help isn't too great, but there's privacy."

She ordered another drink. "Any good-looking men?"

"Oh, yes, loads of eligible bachelors," I said, thinking of the two Indians who had watched me change the tire.

"I think I'll just stick to Hawaii, thanks. Canada sounds a bit rugged for my taste."

"I've been having terrible dreams again," I said, changing the subject.

"I'm not surprised, you idiot. What do you expect, wandering around with savages?"

"They're not savages. They're just a different people with a different way."

"Different is right, waking you up in the middle of the night and scaring you to death. Really! And then they want you to steal something."

"But there's no other way to get the basket," I said, wanting encouragement. "Besides, it's not really stealing. It's a manner of teaching." I twisted the turquoise and antler earring.

"Teaching or whatever, don't you already have enough baskets? How about antique loincloths—something new?"

We went from the restaurant to the County Museum to see the new African exhibit, arrived an hour before closing, and turned into the Ahmanson Gallery. I felt better in the stillness of the room, surrounded by Baule masks from the Ivory Coast.

"Look at this one," Caroline said.

I looked up at the tranquil mask of a young woman, one of those used by the ruling secret society—called the Mmwo—of the Ibo in Nigeria. The face was strong, the hair almost Egyptian in style. The eyes seemed blind of normal vision.

A carving from the Ibo of the Niger Delta had a warrior mounted on the back of a fanged, scaly creature, carrying a rattle and libation cup. The monster he rode was a projection of his own murderous skills, and he held the rattle in his right hand. I remembered that in southwest Nigeria, many tribes devoted themselves to the worship of a man's own right hand, the hand that represents ability as a warrior. But I remembered as well the rattle hanging on Agnes' wall.

I realized I was thinking about what Red Dog looked like. These monstrous primitive figures must have started that train of thought. I hoped that I would never have to see him in person.

Standing by the exit was a carving I liked. On the handle of a fan there was a seated god represented as a double being sharing a single body. I ran my fingers slowly over the worn wood.

"Don't you identify with that?" I asked Caroline.

"No, but I can see how you do."

We laughed. "Let's go home," we said in unison.

At home, later, I curled up in front of the fire with my dog Kona and Peter Matthiessen's *The Snow Leopard*. The room was cozy and warm, and I was exhausted.

I sat staring at the fire blazing in the fireplace. I put my hand on the phone, wishing I could dial Agnes. But if I wanted to talk to her, I would have to travel to Manitoba.

I looked at the several katchina dolls set in shadow on the mantle piece. There is a dualism in the world—everything material has a spiritual counterpart represented by the kachinas. The firelight danced them awake momentarily, their spirits seemed to awaken. Their feathers and brightly painted bodies reminded me of another mysterious world. I watched them. I remembered that Picasso was influenced by magical carvings from Africa and took out a book to look up a passage I remembered:

> I understood what their sculpture did for the Negroes. Why they carved them that way, and not some other way. After all, they weren't Cubists—the Cubists didn't exist yet! Of course, certain men had invented the models, and others had imitated them—isn't that tradition? But all the fetishes did the same thing. They were weapons—to keep people from being ruled by spirits, to help them free themselves. Tools. *Les Demoiselles d'Avignon* must have come that day, not because of the forms, but because it was my first canvas of exorcism! That's why, later on, I painted more pictures like the earlier ones, the *Portrait of Olga*, the other portraits—no one is a sorcerer every hour of the day! How could you live?

Later, in bed, I lay watching the moonlight streaming in through the windowpanes and listening to the familiar hooting of the owl. A cool air blew in and I became oblivious. Then a strange sensation woke me, a rattling noise in my head or next to my ear that became a whirring sound. I realized that the marriage basket was attacking me—I couldn't move. The basket was full of crows, wings fluttering and beating, staring at me with glossy eyes and cawing. The basket was being pushed toward me from directly above. Then it stopped suddenly, close enough to touch, and from its dark form came the ghostly face of a giant kachina man. He had glassy eyes, his mouth hung open, and his body was wildly painted. I screamed and awoke in terror as the phone rang.

"Hello," I answered in a hoarse voice.

"Ho, Lynn, this is Hyemeyohsts Storm."

"Oh, hello. Wait a minute. I'm so glad it's you. I've had another terrible nightmare."

"Tell me about it," he said cheerfully.

I sat up and turned on the light and told him.

"Are you going to Canada?" he asked.

There was a knot in my stomach. Kona hopped on the bed and nervously curled up against me. His body was shaking.

"I don't know yet. But what about my dream?"

"I'm in New Mexico taking care of business," Hyemeyohsts said, ignoring my question. "But I've been thinking about you and now I know why. You must understand that the dreamers have chosen you. Remember the wolf fur I gave you when I drew you the map? Don't ever sleep without it, because powers other than the dreamers will try to harm you. The wolf fur will protect you. As the huntress you are also the hunted. You must understand that will is not a mystery. It is simple. Will dreams the balance and cracks the skull. What are your night visions or your pain but the failure of your will? I have to go now. I leave you within the mirror of creativity and touching the world circle." He hung up.

I looked at the phone, annoyed by the abruptness of the call. What had Hyemeyohsts said—will? The failure of my will? The will to what? I took out a note pad and wrote down his words. By the time I had finished writing, I knew what he had meant. There was a spark smoldering inside of me, trying to ignite, but it was still too weak to do so. I knew that somehow my will was being fed, that it would begin to control and propel me toward a strange destiny. I knew that I was nearing a dark abyss, and that somehow I was going to have to plunge into its inconceivable depth. I cried until I fell asleep again.

The next morning I awoke with swollen eyes, and put the small piece of wolf fur in an old hide medicine pouch that I had collected. I laid the pouch on my night table.

At four that afternoon, Ivan arrived with George and Pamela Helmstead, from Arthur's party, to view what Ivan liked to call "the Beverly Hills wigwam." I spent a long time showing them my art collection. As we moved from one piece to another, I gave a brief history of my experiences in Canada—I couldn't quit talking. The Helmsteads listened politely, but Ivan seemed to be smirking.

We went out on the brick patio to have tea and cookies. The bougainvillea trellised overhead was ignited in color, crimson against the blue sky.

"Why learn to steal a basket, Lynn?" Ivan asked. He took a bite of cookie. "Why not just steal recipes like other women?" He added quickly, "These cookies are delicious."

I said, "I hope you choke on them."

George and Pamela laughed.

"You'd never get the basket out of my bank," George said pompously. "You're not dealing with reputable people up there, you know. You'll lose it. Someone will probably steal it back from you."

I heard myself saying, "Perhaps it's the search and the challenge that interests me—although Agnes said I could literally die trying to do it."

"Could you really be killed?" Pamela asked incredulously.

"That's what Agnes said."

"In that case, forget it. I mean, it's just a basket." Pamela sipped her tea.

"Maybe I'm under some kind of a spell, but I really am fascinated. Besides, it's not just a basket."

"Why can't you go up to Canada and just learn what that woman wants you to do?" Ivan asked. "I'll go along and find out if this so-called medicine woman is a charlatan—how about that?"

"Well, I don't know what to do. Agnes was very explicit that no one was to come with me."

"She's a phony, Lynn," Ivan said, with an air of finality.

We made small talk, finished the tea, and said goodbye. I watched them drive off and afterwards, alone, read a book with a happy ending.

That evening I got in my car to go to La Famiglia, to have dinner with Arnold Schulman. The air was cool, and heavy with the scent of night-blooming jasmine.

La Famiglia is usually just crowded enough to be interesting, and they allow me long hours for talk over dinner. It would sound as though I am forever sitting and eating, but in fact that is the best way to be around people in Los Angeles. In Rome or Paris you can walk out on the streets and be in the mainstream of life. Not so, L.A.

"It's been a while," I said to Arnold after we had been seated. "Have you been away?"

Arnold smiled. "As a matter of fact I've just gotten back from the jungles of Peru. This is going to sound bizarre, but I went to Peru to look for a hallucinogen called ayahuasca. The Indians call it the vine of death, and William Burroughs called it 'the final fix.' I found an Indian guide and went up the Amazon to find a witch doctor I'd heard of, though I'd been told the man was impossible to find, let alone learn from. We hacked our way through the jungle, eaten up by mosquitos and dripping from the humidity. Finally we found the village where he lived—straw huts, about six or seven of them. When we got there, all the people had gone hunting and it was deserted—except for him. There he was, sitting on his pole platform wearing a baseball cap and a Hawaiian shirt, smiling."

"You must have flipped."

"I really did. He looked like an Indian Casey Stengle. Very old. Skinny.

"When the people take the ayahuasca, they leave their bodies. While they're out of the physical body, the witch doctor examines them to see what's wrong, and he heals them. I had hoped to take part in that ceremony."

"So what did you do?"

"I spoke with the man through the guide and he decided I'd take the vine of death sitting across from him on his platform. He was very solemn. By this time it was night."

"Were you scared?"

"Of course. But not as scared as when I got back and found out ayahuasca is about fifty times stronger than acid."

"That's what I've heard, but the difference is the healing properties. Is that right?"

"It'll kill you or heal you, they say."

We laughed. "Arnold, it sounds appalling. So what happened next?"

"Well, first I gave him a bottle of Jack Daniels and some other little things and then we settled ourselves in front of a makeshift shrine. It was hard to see clearly in the darkness. There was only a candle burning. I noticed a statue of the Virgin Mary, carved wooden fetishes, feathers, and small bundles tied with ribbons. There was a hollowed-out gourd set up on sticks, and the old man began to chant over it. Finally he dipped into it with a polished half of a coconut shell, and handed it to me. It smelled and tasted like vomit. I forced it down and handed the cup back, and he took his drink. He said it would last only six or seven hours but when the sun came up on the second day and I was still flying, I knew I was in trouble."

Arnold was laughing, but I wasn't. "What did you learn?" I asked.

"What I learned was really experiential and hard to explain. I flew with amazing speed over peoples' lives—people I know. I could see them interacting and carrying on daily routines. I felt that I saw them in some more important dimension, as if our present reality was artificial."

We were silent for several moments.

"Arnold, you didn't do all that just for a script, did you?"

Arnold folded his napkin and gave me an impish grin.

"No."

"But why would you risk your life? You have it all. You must make a zillion dollars a year. You're even happy."

Arnold reflected for a moment. "Maybe it's like what Nietzsche said. 'That which does not destroy me strengthens me.'"

Arnold was quiet for a moment and then looked at me expectantly. "Okay, let's talk about your experience. Your eyes are going 'tilt.'"

I took a bite of veal and thought for a moment. What had happened in Canada seemed less tangible than taking a drug and having hallucinations for a prescribed length of time.

"Now that I can talk about it, I don't know where to begin. I've been having recurrent dreams about an encounter I had with a medicine woman named Agnes. I'm feeling a bit disoriented."

I went on to tell Arnold parts of the story and how the marriage basket had become an obsession. It must have sounded like a nightmare. "The only thing I have so far to show for my time is the earring. I left it at home, but I'll let you see it sometime. I hope you don't think this is totally absurd, Arnold?"

"Come on, Lynn. What else is there but the search?"

"I guess you're right."

"But some things I still don't understand. What *is* the marriage basket? What does it mean?"

"Well, I can only tell you what Agnes told me." I looked at the mirrors behind Arnold and saw echoes of my own frustration. "Agnes told me that the basket was woven by dreamers and represented an unspeakable void—the womb in woman. It is law that all things must be born in woman, even things invented by men. All the stars were born from the void, and the void is woman. Creation invented the male to balance that. It said, I'll put a man inside of her. In a man is the muse-female. Agnes said that men have taken the void and said it was theirs, and that as a result our mother earth is now in a state of great imbalance."

Arnold stared at me. "Is the basket real or a metaphor?"

"No, as I told you, I saw a photograph of it. The basket is a fact. It is not a metaphor."

"Can I go to Canada with you? I'd love to meet your medicine woman."

"I wish you could come. I'd be much less frightened if you were there."

"Is there any reason I can't go?"

"I was told that the teachings are sacred, and that I can't bring anyone with me."

Arnold looked at me uncertainly and took a sip of espresso. He put the cup down. "I'd much rather deal with Agnes *and* the vine of death than most of the studio heads I know."

We laughed. The conversation lapsed into silence for a moment. I took a deep breath and said, "Arnold, I've been so scared by those dreams. I have to drop this whole dreadful thing—somehow, I don't know how. It's tearing me apart. If I go to Agnes I'm afraid my life as I know it will end. I still have all manner of things to do here. I have a big auction coming up in New York, and so many people are depending on me. I can't just drop everything on a whim and follow an obsession." I grabbed my glass and took a drink.

Arnold looked startled. "Lynn, you can't let this chance go by you. Your dreams are messages. Stop being an idiot and think about what you're saying. Auctions, people depending on you? Your own fear—isn't that the real phantom you have to deal with?"

I felt tears starting to form. "It may kill me, Arnold."

"So what? You have to face it. Go through to the other side. You *have* to go to Canada. You know that."

I simply couldn't admit Arnold was right. "No, I don't know that."

Arnold reached over and touched my hand. "Look, don't you realize how incredible this is for you? You've been handed an incredible gift. Don't question it. Look around at these people—Hollywood's finest."

I took a quick glance at the crowd. In the flattering atmosphere of La Famiglia the diners certainly appeared serene.

"What the hell have they really accomplished in their lives?" Arnold asked, squeezing my hand and smiling. "And what have you really done with yours? But here you are with a reprieve. If you're lucky enough to fall into one of those holes in fate, goddamn it, go with it as far as it takes you."

"Arnold, I thought you wanted me alive."

"Not alive. *Really* alive. You have to find out what this obsession really means," he said. "And I'll bet you'll find out the marriage basket can save you."

"I hope so."

"Get on a plane tomorrow," Arnold said later, as we were leaving. "I can't wait to hear what happens. Let me know as soon as you get back—if you get back."

"Thanks, Arnold," I said, laughing as I kissed him good night.

I drove off resolving to call the airlines when I got home. But as my car moved up Beverly Drive, I started thinking about what I had experienced at the hands of Agnes and Ruby. I wondered if I was just another fool swept up in some kind of hocus-pocus. When I arrived at my house, I sat in my living room weighing all this. I was wearing the turquoise and antler earring. Was I so unaware that I had put it back on when I arrived home? I took it off and studied it carefully. It was the only tangible part of this dream.

After a quick shower I went to bed, purposefully leaving the earring by the sink in the bathroom. I left the light on and dreamed of the marriage basket. I was walking toward it, but when I got there Agnes stood in its place.

"Now you must come. It is time."

"Yes," I answered without hesitation.

Her figure dissolved and I slept peacefully.

In the morning, the earring was on my ear—gouging into my cheek as I awoke. This time I knew for sure that there were non-ordinary events happening. I thought of the dream as I looked at the earring in the palm of my hand. Agnes had said it was a transition object—a bridge from my world to hers.

I picked up the phone and made a reservation to fly back to Canada, and Agnes, immediately.

It is law that all things must be born in woman, even things invented by men.

—Agnes Whistling Elk

Crowley was a welcome sight. I parked in front of the store, cut the engine, got out, and slammed the door. Three small Cree children with black hair and round faces stared at me for a moment and then ran off toward the river.

"Hurry! Hurry!" they called.

Across the street, several old men were sitting on the local post office bench. They used sign language to communicate with one another—I gathered I was the brunt of some private joke. I pretended I didn't notice and pushed my way through the creaking screen door. The papers on the bulletin board rustled, and I stood facing the shelves of cheap food and hardware.

The store owner was behind the front counter by the register, his arms folded over a western shirt embroidered with roses. He did a little nervous dance and spit tobacco juice.

"Where's your tuna fish?" I asked.

"It's right over there." He pointed to the back of the store.

I went around the store collecting groceries—peanut butter, bread, jelly, and so forth.

"You find old Ruby last time you were here?" he asked as I was looking at a can of apple juice.

"Yes, I found her."

His face was passive and he spit tobacco juice again. "I hope you know what you're doing."

"I do."

"I sure hope so." He leaned forward, resting his elbows on the counter. "I don't want to scare you but I'd be careful. Some girls who go out there—I don't mean just white girls—Indians too—lose their marbles. You think they know what they're doing and the next time you see them, they look dead inside. It wouldn't be the first time that's happened. It's a risk fooling around with a woman like Ruby."

"I'm not fooling around with Ruby. The woman I came to see this time is named Agnes."

The man's face drained of color and he practically choked on his tobacco juice. "Agnes Whistling Elk?"

"Yes."

He suddenly looked frightened. "You know her?"

"Yes."

He stood up straight and looked apologetic. "Take this," he said, waving a carton of cigarettes. "I was just kidding about Ruby."

I was dumbfounded at the difference in his behavior. The mere mention of Agnes' name caused this middle-aged Indian to panic. He came around the counter and down the open aisle, still brandishing the carton of cigarettes.

"Here, take this tobacco," he yelled loudly, shoving the cigarettes into my hand.

"I . . . I don't smoke," I stammered.

"Oh, that's all right. Take it anyway—okay?" He seemed insistent and tried to smile.

"Thank you," I said, annoyed. I had absolutely no use for tobacco.

Then I remembered what Hyemeyohsts Storm had said about tobacco being sacred to Native Americans. I put the cigarettes with my other groceries and the owner made his way back behind the counter.

I put the bags of groceries in the trunk, got into the car, and started down the highway. I drove slowly to look at the simple frame houses, the old cars, the decayed buildings.

Ahead, I saw two men walking by the side of the road, the same two who had watched while I changed my tire. I pulled up next to them and rolled down the window.

"Want a lift?" I asked. "Remember me?"

"Sure, we remember you," the taller one said, laughing. They got in and settled into the back seat comfortably. It seemed as if they had expected me to be their driver.

"What are your names?" I asked.

"That's Ben and I'm Drum," said the taller of the pair.

"Ben and Drum, huh? It seems like I'm always running into you."

Silence.

"You guys sure made me mad that time when you wouldn't help me change my tire."

More silence. Ben and Drum weren't very talkative.

"How have you been?" I asked.

"Fine," said Drum.

There was another uncomfortable silence, but I was beginning to enjoy the view. I took a deep breath of fresh air and started to relax.

Drum leaned over the front seat and whispered, "Lynn, stop the car."

"What?" I said, hitting the brakes. "Huh?"

"Look at me," he said. "See me." He put his hand flat underneath his mouth as though he were going to blow dust in my face. "I am looking at the face of a goddess."

"What in hell are you saying?"

"I've never beheld such celestial beauty," he said. His eyes took on a strange glow and he seemed to be blowing the words out at me. This wasn't a come-on—his expression was impersonal. He began speaking in a rhythm that sounded familiar.

"This isn't Cree, Lynn. I am speaking a language of long ago. Bring your eyes into the center of my words."

Once, when I was eight years old, I watched a man in a pet

shop feed a gerbil to a snake. The little creature froze just before the snake struck, recognizing and submitting to its death. Drum's indescribable words were the answer to that riddle and now I, too, was submitting.

I used all my will to get out of that state. I started to yell.

"Please, stop! Stop!"

"Stop what?" asked Drum. His eyes changed.

"Green light, lady," Ben said.

I was shivering. I started off down the road again in a series of jerks and jolts. Drum sat back in his seat and ignored me.

"Where are you going?" Ben asked.

I was still trying to clear my head. "To Agnes Whistling Elk's place. I have to leave my car at Ruby Plenty Chiefs' cabin and walk in."

Both Ben and Drum laughed derisively.

"No, you don't," Ben said. "There's a back road to Whistling Elk's."

"Where is it? Agnes never told me about a back road."

Drum leaned forward with his elbows over the seat. "Of course, she wouldn't tell you. She wouldn't give you the right time of day. She's a witch. Everyone knows that."

"The road is right up there," Ben said, pointing. "Just turn left and it will take you a hundred yards from her cabin."

"She didn't mention it," I said.

"That old hag," said Drum, still resting forward on the seat. "A person like you doesn't belong out here. Where are you from, anyway?"

"Beverly Hills, California."

Drum smiled. "Isn't that where all those movie stars live?"

"Some."

"Are you a movie star?" Ben asked.

"No."

Drum sat back. "We think you ought to go back home."

"Why do you say that?"

"Well, the last white chick that came out here was found staked to an ant hill."

"Very funny," I said.

"Stop. We want off at that fork."

I pulled the car over and stopped. Ben and Drum started to climb out. Drum paused with his foot on the ground outside the car.

"We live right down that path," he said. "If you need any help or anything, come over and get us. We'll fix old Agnes for you."

Ben laughed. "Yeah, we'll fix her good."

"Well, thank you," I said. "If she turns out to be a witch, I'll be right over."

"We work for a white guy," Drum said. "He's pretty smart. You ought to meet him. He likes pretty women." He slammed the door. "They like him, too," he called as an afterthought.

"See you around the res," called Ben. "Don't take any wooden buffalo."

Together they walked down the path leading into the distant grassy hills. I sat there for several minutes with my motor running, a queasy sensation in my stomach. I tried to grapple with what had happened. Some wild-eyed Indian suddenly started talking crazy, and I nearly fainted and felt very close to death—too close. The incident was chilling.

I gave a sigh and drove off slowly down the dirt road. The sun was warm through the windshield. The road wound through green and rolling hills and dead-ended at a sheer rock cliff. I didn't see a cabin anywhere, but there was a narrow path leading off around the hillside and I followed it. Perhaps this was not really a road to Agnes' at all.

Just below me, though, was the tin roof of Agnes' cabin, smoke curling up from the chimney. I started to run down the hill, almost skipping, came around the corner of the cabin, and ran right into her. She was glaring at me, her face dark—angry. I stopped dead in my tracks.

"Those two men you picked up were Red Dog's apprentices. You should have told me that they saw you last time."

"How on earth was I supposed to know they were anybody special?"

"Ben and Drum smoked you for power and found that you have none, not yet anyway. You're more stupid than I thought. You've made your first mistake."

"How did you ever know I picked them up?"

Without answering, Agnes spun around and walked into the cabin. I followed, trying to apologize. She jerked out a chair and pointed. "Sit."

I sat down.

The table was covered with various herbs, which Agnes began to tie in bundles. "You might as well have gone over to Red Dog's and announced your arrival. It's a good thing you're wearing your earring or they would have killed you."

I was astounded. "How would they have killed me?"

"Sorcerers never kill anybody. They make people kill themselves."

"How?" I asked.

"If a sorcerer were to pick up a gun and shoot you, he would lose power. They either make you kill yourself or make someone else do it."

I told her about the crazy experience in the car with Drum. "Can you explain what happened?" I asked.

"Drum was remembering you. He went back to one of your previous life circles, or incarnations."

"What are you talking about, Agnes?"

"Drum tried to jerk you across before your time. You would never have come back—you're too weak. Your earring talked to that remembering so you wouldn't go across. You were lucky this time."

"You mean Drum could kill me just by talking to me?"

"Yes, and he very nearly succeeded. You have to wake up and keep your eyes alert. The dreamers must think you have power, but I can't imagine what it might be."

My enthusiasm for this adventure was dissipating.

Agnes got up and hung the herb bundles on various nails over the sink, dipped a tin cup into an open bucket of water, and took a drink. Then she turned and faced me.

"Tell me exactly what has taken place between you and Red Dog's apprentices, starting from the beginning."

I told her everything I could remember about the first meeting, when Ben and Drum walked up as I was fixing the tire. I also remembered more details of our second meeting. Agnes' face was expressionless.

"And why didn't you tell me about the road to your cabin?" I demanded.

"Tell you. Didn't you know? We're going to have to smarten you up," she said, shaking her head.

When we went out to unload my things, I noticed that one of the car doors was open.

"I don't ordinarily leave the car door open," I said. "That's strange."

We walked around to the back of the car. I popped open the trunk lid.

"What's that?" Agnes asked, her hands on her hips. She coolly surveyed my two suitcases, makeup bag, air mattress, sleeping bag, and the three bags of groceries. She picked up two of the bags, the carton of cigarettes poking out of the top underneath her chin. She walked quickly down the path, and I followed her with my two suitcases. I dropped my things off inside and returned for the remaining things. When I got back, Agnes had the two half gallons of chocolate ice cream sitting on the table. The containers sat in a large brown puddle. Agnes gave me a curious look.

"How was I supposed to know it would melt so fast?"

"You wasichu," she said.

Agnes got a spoon and ate some of the liquid ice cream. When she finished, she threw the cartons out her door.

"Pretty good," she said. "Dogs will like it."

"Don't you have a freezer or any ice box?"

"I had a big one this winter."

She blew up my air mattress. The rubber inflated quickly. When it was full, she placed it on the floor facing in the same direction as her bed. She then unrolled my sleeping bag and smoothed it out on top of the air mattress. The grocery bags were emptied and

67

the food and canned goods were stacked neatly on the shelf. I wanted to help but I knew I would be in the way. When Agnes was finished working, she took her mackinaw off a wall peg and put it on. "I want you to drive me over to Ruby's house so I can get my rattle. We'll bring it back here and I'll work on you. My rattle has some medicine power. I can see a problem in you and I need the rattle to fix it."

But the car wouldn't start. The engine turned over, but it wouldn't catch.

"Looks like you walk," Agnes said matter-of-factly. Indians all seemed to look straight ahead when they were in cars. "You can go get it tomorrow. I hope it's not too late then. You need that rattle power pretty quick. You should go to Ruby's and get it now, but it's not safe to go at night. Besides, you're not used to the dark, are you?"

"Me? Walk around here at night? No way." The prospect was frightening.

"Well come on. Get out," she said.

We walked back to the cabin. Agnes didn't take off her mackinaw. "You'll have to stay here alone tonight. I have to go to a medicine meeting. You can start off for Ruby's in the morning when I get back."

"Alone—here?"

"Yes, go to sleep. Remember to keep the door bolted—not that it would do any good. Red Dog prowls around here at night every once in a while."

I shuddered.

"I wish we could have gotten my rattle," Agnes said gravely. "Be alert."

I stood at the window and watched her disappear up the hill. If anything happened I had no way of getting out of here, except on foot. I lit a kerosene lamp, glad I remembered to bring books and a journal with me. I washed my makeup off in a pan of water, undressed, and slid into my down bag. The lamp was close to my head, and I turned to the day's entry in my journal and began to write.

After a while, I became aware of the scent of smoke. The stove was making a dull hissing sound. I put the notebook down, and shuddered inside the warm bag. My thoughts were running away with me again.

I realized that if Red Dog were really to burst into the cabin, I would be trapped in the sleeping bag. I got up, put my clothes back on, and sat at the table on a rickety chair. The dark windows reflected the owl wing and rattle hanging on the opposite wall. Occasionally, the northern lights would stream across the sky, then a great glow would hover, like the distant flamelight of a city under siege. The trees next to the cabin, dark frightful shapes, swayed and rubbed in an ominous dance. An owl, perched high on a naked twisted branch, hooted. I could see his feathery silhouette.

The wind was picking up outside and an occasional groaning noise vibrated through the cabin. Every once in a while something would fall on the tin roof—it must have been a pine cone. I jumped with each sharp sound. Several dark shadows in the room lurked ever closer as the northern lights began to fade.

I had always loved it when the lights flared up, but not now.

I lit the other lantern, stomped around and acted cheerful, and washed my face again in cold water.

"What in the hell is that?" I said out loud.

There had been a snarling noise, then a sound like a large animal crashing through the underbrush. I stripped off my clothes in four seconds flat and jumped into the protective womb of my sleeping bag. Not satisfied, I got out quickly and placed the two lanterns on either side of my sleeping bag. They were running out of fuel, but I was too afraid to stay out of the sleeping bag any longer to look for more. A wolf, or coyote, started howling in the distance—his eerie song seemed to be getting nearer. The wind was rattling the tin roof—I thought it was going to blow off. The cabin shook and groaned, and I thought I saw the flash of a man's face looking at me through the window. I heard a crunch like the bones of a bird being eaten by a dog.

Both lanterns started to spit and flicker. "Agnes!" I cried.

The lanterns went out within a minute of each other. The

northern lights streaked across the walls, and two eyes glimmered from underneath Agnes' bed. I pulled the bag-womb over my head and fainted into sleep.

"I knew you needed that power rattle. Get up, you idiot. The door was wide open. Those fiends took your clothes."

I started awake.

Agnes gave a fit of diabolical laughter. "They took everything you own. They took your clothes. They took the groceries. They took everything."

Light shafted through the windows. It was early morning. I jumped to my feet and stood there naked.

"Who?" I bawled. "Took what?"

My two suitcases were gone. My Gucci bag lay open on the floor with the lining ripped out. Credit cards and money were strewn everywhere. Even my makeup case was missing.

"Oh, no," I moaned.

"At least they knew better than to take anything of mine."

I sat down at the table, held my head in my hands, and realized that a large swatch of hair had been cut away from my bangs. I ran over to the tiny mirror over the wash basin.

Agnes slapped her thigh and laughed.

"Agnes, look at my hair. It's ruined."

Agnes was grinning.

"Who cut it? What could have happened last night?" I felt like a naked child standing in a roomful of strangers. Tears ran down my cheeks.

Agnes handed me an old sweatshirt, an enormous pair of ragged jeans, and a length of rope to hold the pants up. My sneakers had been under my pillow, and I was glad to see they were still there.

"Why?" I asked, looking up from tying a bow.

"They counted coup on you. That was Red Dog's way of humiliating you." She came over and lifted a handful of hair. "If Red Dog did that to me, he would have honor. With you, maybe he just did it for fun." She let my hair fall.

"Red Dog?" I asked. I stared at Agnes with wide eyes.

"Yeah, that damn pup. I'm going to leave some poison out for him one of these days."

"You mean Red Dog came in here in the middle of the night and stole everything?" I looked at the solid iron lock on the door.

"Well, at least he didn't cut your throat. Anyone else would have."

"This is awful." I cried at my predicament. "I could kill myself."

"Why don't you?" she asked seriously.

I was pouting. "You wouldn't care if I did, would you?"

"I would care because you would fail the dreamers. Otherwise . . . " She shrugged her shoulders. "You can either kill yourself or face facts. The facts are you're stupid. Here, sit down and have some tea."

I was furious. "Okay Agnes, everyone keeps talking about the dreamers. The least you can do is fill me in. What or who is a dreamer? I think I'm entitled to some answers."

"Yes, we may as well get started. Listen carefully, Lynn, because these are secrets." She made herself comfortable in her chair. There was a subtle change in her demeanor. "A dreamer is one who knows how to enter the sacred round and exit at will."

"What do you mean by sacred round?"

"The sacred rounds, and there are seven, are controlled by the katchina powers. The first round is normal everyday life, the world you live in and the way you normally perceive it. The second round is sleep. The third round is where the dreamers go." Agnes thought for a moment and said, "I have to translate from Indian. It is called walking through the gateway between the worlds. Understand this, you only go between the worlds. If you were in them you would be spirit, and that would be what we call death."

"In other words, the dreamers have come to me in the second round and have taken me between the worlds?"

"That is right, but you don't have the power yet to remember anything but your dreams."

"But why are they coming to me?"

"Because consciously or unconsciously you have made a bid for power."

"In other words, be careful what you ask for?" I thought to myself of all the years I had spent aimlessly studying mysticism.

"Girl," Agnes said, pouring the tea and changing to a more cheerful attitude. "Red Dog knows you. He'll probably humiliate you again. He wants you to go back where you came from. You better go get that rattle from Ruby Plenty Chiefs before they do more than humiliate you."

We drank the tea and ate something.

"Do you remember the way to Ruby's?" Agnes asked.

"Yes," I said. "How could I forget?"

"Now that you see what can happen, do you want to go back?"

"No," I said angrily.

"Well, you'd better watch your ass. Red Dog wants to whoop it up and go to town on you. Counting coup is nothing to what he could do to you."

I swallowed hard and cleared my throat. "Will you walk with me?"

Agnes crossed her arms. "Get going."

I left the cabin and started walking at a fast pace to Ruby's, surprised at how much of the terrain I had forgotten. I was aware of the absurdity of my outfit and laughed at myself as a gust of wind pulled at my faded denims and the old fabric billowed around my ankles. The rope hung down from my gathered waist and flicked the back of my legs. I thought about my oldest friend Cyrena and how she would laugh if she could see me, but I couldn't let my mind wander. I had to keep my head clear and try to learn something. I ran along the path near the flowering bank of the creek. I could hear the sound of the swirling water and catch glimpses of sunlight streaming through the poplar trees. I could still smell wood-smoke on me. I wore it like perfume.

I walked and jogged for three solid hours until Ruby's cabin came into view in the distance. I stopped, my stomach turning over.

As I started walking again, I heard the faint trilling sound of a flute being carried on the wind. As I approached, the sound grew louder.

A frail young girl was sitting on Ruby's porch, blowing into the instrument. Her hair was jet black and hung down to her waist, and I realized she was beautiful. I waved at her but got no response. I shouted, but she continued to play her flute.

"That's a pretty sound," I said, when I got to the porch.

The girl continued to blow on the flute.

"I said that's a pretty sound."

She blew the same notes.

"Hey!" I said.

I knelt in front of her and looked into her eyes but she kept playing the same maddening notes. I waved my hands in front of her beautiful oval face. Her dark eyes were vacant and did not track. Her body was rigid as a stone. I remembered what the store owner in Crowley had said about the girls who visited Ruby.

Ruby burst out of her cabin door. "Stop bothering her. That won't do any good!"

I shrank back.

"Don't talk to July. She doesn't understand you."

I cringed. The girl looked straight ahead, playing the same notes over and over.

"What do you want here, wasichu?"

"Agnes sent me to get her rattle."

"What rattle?"

"She said she needed it to help me."

"I don't have her damned rattle. Why didn't Agnes come to pick it up?"

"I don't know."

Ruby looked at me disgustedly. "She must mean the rain rattle. She wants to borrow it. I don't know if I should give it to you. It's plenty dangerous."

"Agnes said she needed her rattle," I stammered.

"Well, are you sure you want to risk it?"

"Risk what?"

"Death. What else is there to risk? If the rain rattle touches the mother earth in a certain way, you're dead. If she's not comforted by one-who-knows-how by sundown, she will call up spirits to kill you. If I entrust you with my rattle and you make a mistake, nothing in the world could stop your death. Are you sure you want to risk it?"

"Agnes told me to get it."

Plainly Ruby was unhappy with the situation. I noticed as I looked at her frown that she was not looking directly at anyone. I remembered she was blind. Now there were two people who didn't seem to see me.

July blew the notes on her flute and Ruby stared off into the distance. "I'll get you the rattle," she said. She went back into the cabin, then returned after a good while.

"Here she is," she said, and threw the rattle at me. It was weathered-brown in color and about nine inches long, with designs carved into the handle. The bulb was about the size of a tennis ball, and I could hear something like seeds rolling around inside. It was forbidding.

As I was examining it, Ruby's hand shot out and felt my head. "It looks like you're bald here," she said. She started to laugh. "Who in hell would count coup on you?"

"Red Dog."

She broke into a fit of hysterical laughter, slapped her leg, and doubled over.

"Red Dog's a rough man," she said, wiping her eyes. "Listen, I am doing you a big favor by loaning Agnes my rattle. Now I want you to do me a little favor. Take July back with you and tell Agnes I said to watch her for a few days." July was still blowing the flute.

"Sure, I'd be happy to, Ruby," I said. "But does she ever stop playing that flute?"

"Never. And don't dare take it away from her. That would finish her. She's driving me batty. That's why I want Agnes to watch her."

The flute playing went on.

"Can you get her to come with me?"

Ruby jerked July to her feet and spoke to her in Cree.

"She'll go with you," she said.

Ruby brought me a peanut butter sandwich and a glass of juice, explaining to me what to do. No matter what happened, the rain rattle was to be in Agnes' hands by dark. I said goodbye, and with July following along behind me playing the flute, we struck out for Agnes' cabin.

I clutched the rattle to my breast with my cupped hands. I was tired, but afraid to rest. The sky was silver blue, the day no longer cold. I walked slowly, carefully, each step important. July progressed at the same deliberate pace—no faster, no slower—piping the same notes.

It was mid-afternoon and I had plenty of time to get to Agnes'. I was beginning to suspect both Ruby and Agnes of conspiring to use me as their village idiot. How could a rattle have power? If the rain rattle could kill me if it touched the ground in the wrong way, why had Ruby thrown it at me on the porch?

The music was getting on my nerves, and my muscles were beginning to ache. Even I was not that gullible. I knew more about power objects than anyone else I dealt with. I had owned, bought, and sold many of them. There was magic in their beauty, as there was in all beauty, and that was their sole power.

After an hour, I was getting giddy. July kept playing and I stood for a few minutes, waiting for her to catch up. The wind was picking up, leaves and sand were stirring. July was walking as though in a trance, stumbling every once in a while but never looking down at her feet, just following. She never missed a note. There was no way to shut her off.

The flute was irritating me, and I began to shake the rattle. I juggled the handle back and forth between my right and left hands, then, as July and I made our way across the craggy terrain, started flipping it in the air and catching it. Those old women weren't going to make a fool out of me. There was a slim chance that I would drop it, but not much. I was tempted to drop the rattle on purpose.

Then I stopped, frightened. I remembered the bald spot on my head, and gave Ruby the benefit of the doubt.

A crow flew directly over my left shoulder, landed in a tree, folded its wings, and settled on a branch. July stopped walking and stood at the base of the tree, continuing to pipe.

"Come on, July," I yelled.

July didn't respond to my command.

The crow ruffled its feathers.

"Oh, will you please come on!"

It was getting late. Ruby had said that if I didn't get the rattle to Agnes by sundown, the spirit of the rain rattle would destroy me. July might stand at that tree forever, and I couldn't leave her. Perhaps she was drawn to the crow and if I could make the bird fly away, she would leave with me.

I looked around and found several stones, careful not to let the rattle touch the ground. I reared back and hurled, and the rock whizzed right by the crow. Again and again I threw, but the crow didn't budge. When the rocks came close, he leapt into the air, settled back, and cawed angrily. I gave up.

"We have to get to Agnes'," I said, jerking July by the arm.

Her body was rigid.

"July," I yelled. "Don't you understand? We have to go!"

She kept blowing the flute, her jet eyes vacant.

The crow cawed overhead.

"Damn you," I shouted. "Move!" I pulled on her arm with a great tug and fell backward. The rattle bounced out of my arms and onto the bare ground. I thought I was going to die.

A shadow of darkness fell. A cool wind licked over me and a loud clap of thunder rolled overhead. Rain began falling, pelting me in cold drops. A shard of lightning split the sky. I looked up at dark clouds blotting out the sunlight. The cloudburst had happened so quickly, I suspected my mind was playing tricks on me. July's cheeks puffed as she played. The crow strutted on the limb and flew away, and it was as if July had been released. I was able to turn her toward Agnes' house, even though now I was in a daze. I felt vaguely drunk and I was shivering. My heart was beating quickly and I picked up the rattle. The wind was strong. Water dripped down from the trees, but the rain had stopped. The clouds puffed gray and angry.

Not long after leaving the tree, we passed out from underneath the dark clouds. The sky was cloudless except over the narrow island of ground where I had dropped the rattle. There, a wedge of ominous gray-black haze divided the sky.

July's flute sang the endless notes behind me.

At last we got to Agnes'. The red rays of the sun lit the horizon.

Agnes came out to meet us. "Give me the rain rattle quick," she ordered. "You nearly died."

My heart jumped violently. I handed her the rattle and she ran into the cabin with it. July trudged to the porch and sat down with her back against a post. She kept blowing the flute.

The moment I entered the cabin, Agnes said, "Go get me some water from the stream." She handed me a bucket.

I soon returned with the bucket full of water.

"Eat," Agnes said.

I sat down at the table and began eating. Agnes sat down across from me. "Tell me exactly what happened to you today, without omitting anything."

After I told her, Agnes stood up. With one deft movement, she seized me by the throat and pulled me forward. I was surprised at her great strength. She twisted my face around so that I was staring at the basket containing the rain rattle on top of her dresser. "Look at her," she said, slowly loosening her grip. "Don't look away from her. Tell her you have respect and mean it."

"You mean talk to the rattle?"

"Yes. You have offended her."

I was so unnerved by Agnes' sudden violence, I virtually screamed, "I'm sorry. I have respect."

"You're not sorry," Agnes said. "You simply have respect."

"I have respect," I said.

"Tomorrow you can go back to Ruby's and get the right rattle. You brought the rain rattle. I wanted the mother rattle. The mother rattle is a turtle-shell rattle."

"You mean I have to walk all that way again?"

"Tomorrow. Right now you better go to bed."

I fell asleep to those solitary notes on the flute.

Those are dead babies that haven't been born yet. They're inside you, always crying. They have been crying for a thousand years, where the wheels of darkness spin forever.

—Ruby Plenty Chiefs

I started to wake up, but felt so cozy and warm that I lingered in my comfortable dreamworld. It was too early to get up.

Tap tap tap tap—

I became aware of a noise like a loose shingle caught in the wind. I kept thinking the noise would stop.

Tap tap tap tap—

I finally opened my eyes and sat up with a groan. My muscles ached, there were twinges of pain in my legs from all the walking I had been doing, and I felt cramps. I looked around the cabin for Agnes. No one was there.

Tap tap tap tap—

There it was again.

I looked out the irregular wood windows. There was a large black crow with glossy wings and brilliant eyes tapping on the window with a large beak, cocking his head from side to side, and peering straight at me.

Tap tap tap tap—

Was the crow pleading with me to let him inside? Birds were supposed to be afraid of people—certainly afraid of coming inside a house.

Tap tap tap tap—

Now he seemed impatient.

Suddenly the cabin door burst open and Agnes came in cradling two logs in her arms. One at a time, she fed them to the fire in the stove.

Tap tap tap tap—

She turned and leaned forward, making a funny clicking noise with her tongue. Then she opened the window and laughed at the bird, which paraded up and down the window sill, puffing out his breast and strutting like a gentleman. He made what seemed like a courtly bow in my direction, cawed reproachfully, and flew to the table in the center of the room. I laughed. I was delighted with this clown.

"This is Crow," said Agnes. "Lynn, meet Crow."

"Nice to meet you," I said. "But I think he looks displeased with me."

"He is. He wanted in for breakfast," Agnes said, turning to Crow and holding out some jerky. Crow seemed more docile as he took a peck.

I got out of my sleeping bag, pulled on my baggy clothes, and joined Agnes and our visitor for breakfast. As we sipped our coffee and ate, we gave bits of fried bread and bacon to him that seemed to make him happy. He seemed to be an appropriate guest.

"This old bandit has been coming here for breakfast for many years," Agnes said. "He has a bigger appetite than I do."

I had forgotten about July, but the bleeting, mournful notes of the flute interrupted the stillness of the morning.

"Oh, no," I said. "Here we go again."

Agnes nodded her head in agreement, and we both started laughing. July was getting on both our nerves.

Crow flew to the windowsill. He strutted a moment and cawed.

"I am full," Agnes said to him.

Crow cawed again and flew away.

"How could you be full on one piece of fried bread and a strip of bacon?" I asked. "I'm certainly not full."

"It is an expression among my people. It means, 'I have eaten. I am full.' It has nothing to do with food. We don't go around thanking each other for things. There is only one to thank, the noble Great Spirit. It means I am full inside for what we have shared. I feel good. We have only one gift, and that is to choose our death. You say thank you in your world. Thank you is a lie, and I advise you never to say it again. You may say it as a ritual, but never mean thank you to any man—it robs you of power. There is only one exception. When you truly see the Great Spirit in another—then you may address that Spirit in thanks and celebration. Otherwise, forget it."

"But I've been taught . . . "

"I don't care what you've been taught," Agnes said, cutting me off. "You've been taught wrong."

I pondered her words as I took my last bite of fried bread.

"Do you know how to ride horseback?" Agnes asked abruptly.

"Yes, I sometimes ride horses. Why do you ask?"

Agnes was moving around the cabin, tidying up. "You must go get the rattle from Ruby immediately. Today, I will go with you a short distance. We will ride together."

I was thrilled. I quickly cleared off the table.

"I didn't realize there were horses here," I said, walking with Agnes out into the crisp northern air. "Where are they? I haven't seen one horse."

"There is much you haven't seen, Lynn."

Agnes set some jerky down near July and whispered something in her ear. July continued to play. Her eyes were still glassy, her body rigid and cold. She seemed so slight and lonely, and the notes seemed like a bird's call for help—or else a warning. She seemed to be playing with a new sadness.

"She will eat later," Agnes said.

She motioned for me to follow her, and we walked down the trail leading to Ruby's. After a short while, we veered off to the south and the going was more difficult. We followed along a tributary of the stream, the water reflecting a translucent blue-green color. All around us and along the banks were rich pockets of fragrant clover and grass.

"The grass is lush this spring," Agnes said. "It is good for the horses."

I nodded in agreement.

Rabbits were everywhere, turning and dodging as we came upon them, giving tiny squeals as they raced off to hide up in the rocks. I followed Agnes through a shaded depression within the trees and out into a lush meadow.

"This is the south pasture," she said.

She handed me one of the two hackamores she had been carrying over her right shoulder. It was beautiful. It seemed to be braided horsehair—black and white—with what looked like elk antler conchos.

Three well fed horses, two chestnut geldings and a pinto mare, stood grazing down near the creek. All three looked up as we approached, then resumed feeding. They let us walk right up to them, and Agnes patted one of the geldings on the neck. His nostrils flared and he pawed the ground.

"You take the mare. She's gentle and sure-footed, and you may ride her whenever you like. She needs the exercise."

We put the hackamores on and led the horses over to a knee-high rock. Agnes rubbed her gelding's forehead, grabbed the mane on the right side, and swung up on his back. Her agility surprised me.

"Well Agnes, if you can do it, I can do it."

I took the mare's mane on the left side and leapt upwards, but my feet hit the horse mid-belly and I landed flat on my back. The ground was hard.

Agnes was towering above me, sitting bareback on her gelding, laughing.

I picked myself up. The pinto eyed me sleepily, obviously wondering what this "white-eyes" was doing. Again I jumped, and again I slammed to the ground. After another try, I gave up.

"Do it the easy way," Agnes said.

I led the horse over to the rock and stepped up, slipping onto her back.

Agnes glanced at me and broke into laughter again.

"Very funny," I said. And then I asked, "Why do you mount on the right side?"

"Because not so long ago, we Indians carried our medicine shields on the left side."

We rode back toward the trail, taking our time. Mounted on her gelding, her moccasins dangling down, Agnes was striking. She seemed to have tremendous vitality, and her braids blew back in the blustery wind. The horses, which still had their thick winter coats, were docile and well mannered. They were unshod, but their hooves were in good shape and their bodies powerfully muscled. Somebody must have been riding them fairly often.

I swayed from side to side with the gait and relaxed into the quiet morning. We walked our horses along in the sunshine, then cantered across a canyon floor and up into a cradle of rocks, still heading south. The horses' nostrils flared and their ears pricked up at a small herd of grazing cattle below us.

All around us birds were chirping, and above the wild geese honked driving up north. A soft whirl of wind rolled by, and we descended toward the cows. We rode to the far edge of the draw, dismounted in a patch of deep, sweet clover, and let the horses graze.

We sat down and took out our smoked fish and bread. It was a beautiful wilderness area of forests and peaks, with the misting clouds lending a gentle moisture to the air. I tore off a piece of bread and began to chew.

Agnes turned. Her face was red-brown against the green, windy day. "Lynn, what do you believe in?"

I was surprised by the abrupt question.

"What do I believe in?"

"Yes, tell me." She smiled at me with a special glint in her eyes.

"Well, I believe in being honest."

Agnes laughed softly. She placed a small rock on the earth in front of me. "Go on," she said. "What else?"

"I believe in being good at what I do."

Giggling, Agnes placed another rock alongside the other one.

I went on to describe to her all of my important political and ethical values. By the time I had finished, there was quite a large mound of rocks.

"What does that mean?" I asked, indicating the pile.

"Those rocks represent each of your beliefs. There is the hoop of the world and the hoop of the self. Your hoops are like nests that surround you—very comforting. But you must recognize the existence of such safe nests. You must see that you sit on those rocks as if they were eggs and you were the mother hatching them. You must see that you are not free because you will never leave your nest of self-ignorance." Agnes pointed to the rocks. "There is your nest. You can spend the rest of your life hatching that if you want to. Those eggs will be the boundaries of your experience."

She toed the edge of the rockpile with her moccasins. "There is one egg that you would do well to hatch—one that is in harmony with the Great Spirit. It is the sacred rock at the center of the hoop. Hatch the sacred rock and you will hatch the queen bird that rips her talons through all the barriers to perception. Whether you believe me or not, hatch the idea that the hoop of the self is also the hoop of the universe. For you are the queen bird that soars on forever, limitless, and have no boundaries. Only the queen bird builds a true nest, without separations."

She picked up one of the rocks. "This is that part of you that believes in being honest. Yet only one who has shattered the egg of truth and falsehood can be honest. You mother that egg as though it contained a precious child—you brood over counterfeit eggs. Can you throw these children away one by one?"

"No," I said. "My beliefs represent who I am. They represent a kind of truth to me. How could I throw them away?"

"You better. You must realize that you are not free. Walk the sacred path and hatch the limitless egg."

"I will try," I said.

"Say 'my beliefs are not necessarily true, even though I think they are.' "

I repeated the statement and felt confused. I looked at the pile of rocks and felt its dark mass within me.

"Okay," Agnes said, jumping to her feet. "One thing that interests me very much is your political views. I am an organizer, myself. Come on. Let's go organize. There are some important issues that need to be discussed. I want to make the world a better place to live."

I followed her across the field. Agnes walked aggressively toward the herd of cattle, climbed on a boulder, and cleared her throat—I couldn't imagine what she was up to. She flung her arms open wide, and her voice became the commanding voice of a radio announcer or sideshow huckster.

"Cows of the world, unite! You have nothing to lose but your chains."

The cows munched the grass and didn't even look up.

Agnes continued, "Hear me or you will perish. Don't you know that they will eat you? There is a sinister plot afoot."

I sat down cross-legged in the grass—very attentive, unlike the cows surrounding me. Their chewing became more pronounced as Agnes went on pontificating. I could almost hear the cheers of an unseen audience and see the placards of a teeming political rally.

"Brothers and sisters, no one recognizes the debt we owe you!"

I had to move out of the path of an industriously grazing cow.

"You share and give away, asking little in return. I'm asking you the most crucial question in your life." Agnes paused, dramatically swayed on her podium, and tucked her chin in to emphasize the weightiness of her stature. She was a perfect caricature of a blustering politician. I was laughing uncontrollably.

"Do you know the two-leggeds are going to eat you? Cows of the world, lend me your ears." Agnes made a magnanimous gesture.

"You're asleep to the conspiracy around you. Where are your great bovine leaders?" She held her clenched fist in the air and shook it, an expression of great intensity on her face. "You have no hope unless you listen to me. Listen well to what I am going to tell you. Don't you know they are going to eat you?"

A cow mooed, as if dimly inspired.

"Cows of the world, we can build an empire free of oppression, working together, marching together." Perched on a slab of granite amidst a wild field of cattle and piles of manure, Agnes raised both arms as if reacting to a cheering multitude. Tears of laughter ran down my cheeks.

"There is one leader and one leader only," Agnes yelled to a make-believe standing ovation. "The two-leggeds have told you they are more intelligent, but what is a puny two-legged beside your great strength? It's clear to me you need a new chief, and I've brought her here for you today." So saying, Agnes bowed and offered me the rock podium. She sat down, grinning roguishly.

"First, you must realize that you are in danger," I said pompously. Then I got down on my knees—pleading. "You have no awareness of the seriousness of your situation. I'm your savior." I paused for recognition and went on. "If we organize, we have a slim chance at a coup d'etat. If you recognize your great strength, as Agnes has told you, you can be the very lords of the earth."

I knelt there, my arms outstretched. For a moment, I really wanted them to understand. I felt that gulf between truth and ignorance. A curious cow lumbered over and nosed around my legs, then gave my backside a strong butt with her nose. I was off balance just enough to tumble head first into the clover and dried cow manure. The movement was so surprisingly aggressive, and unsuspected, that I turned my head quickly to be sure the cow wasn't coming after me. But she turned away when she saw I had nothing of interest to eat and went back to grazing. The whole scene was too much, and I collapsed next to Agnes.

We rolled around in the tall grass, laughing. The playful roughness of the old woman at once scared and delighted me, and I lost myself in the dense odor of earth and growing things. I spread my hands in the dirt, fist out, like a spatula, as I sat up. It was moist to the touch. Mud and particles of rock clung to my fingers over the contours of my hands, and I had the impulse to cover my face with the wet clay and wallow in the damp, mellow spot. Agnes put out her hand, grasped mine, and pulled me up. She shook her head and laughed at me until tears rolled down her cheeks. Arm in arm, we giggled and stumbled across the rock-strewn meadow like a couple of drunks—bumping shoulders and pretending to lose our balance. I felt intoxicated.

We caught up with the horses and mounted again. I had to use a rock for help. Without warning, Agnes reined her gelding around, toward the cows.

"Help me round up the cattle and drive them to the other end of the pasture," she yelled, and galloped away.

I followed in hot pursuit.

In a matter of minutes, the fat cows, bawling their irritation, were loping in the correct direction.

"The rocks!" I cried out to Agnes.

The cows were going to trample my pile of rocks, my belief structures. I saw them fly in all directions as the herd stampeded right through them. Then I spun my mare around and trampled through the ruin myself. The rocks were scattered, and I pulled in the reins to wait for Agnes. She nodded her head approvingly, a happy glint in her eyes.

"Well, Lynn, do you feel funny now?"

"Yes, I feel funny."

We rode in silence to the end of the meadow. The cattle, after milling around for a short time, resumed their lackadaisical grazing.

"I'm going back to July now," Agnes said. She nodded toward Ruby's cabin, reined her horse in the opposite direction, and trotted off down the trail. "Remember, it's the mother rattle," she called over her shoulder.

I had spent much of the day with Agnes. I knew there was little time to get to Ruby's and back home before dark.

I hope the moon is bright tonight, I thought.

I trotted west down the trail and up over the hill, putting myself out of view of the cows. I decided to call my mare "Paint."

"Git up, Paint."

She had a lovely soft gait that I was thankful for, but I knew I would be sore tomorrow. This trail was becoming familiar. What had been a wilderness zone of terror now appeared clear and ordered. Even the magpies that had so frightened me seemed more playful. Paint was able and willing to keep up her trot—really more like a running walk—endlessly. I gave myself to her rhythmic gait, and we formed a fairly coherent unit.

In what seemed a short time, I arrived before Ruby's cabin. I swung my leg over Paint's ample rump and gingerly slid to the ground. When I looked up, Ruby was standing in the doorway.

"Well, now what?" she demanded.

"I've come this time for the mother rattle," I said. "Yesterday you gave me the wrong rattle."

Ruby glared at me. "I didn't give you the wrong rattle. Agnes has the mother rattle," she said indignantly. "What would I want with the mother rattle?" Her hands were on her hips, and her red skirt was blowing in the breeze.

"Ruby, don't joke with me. I rode all the way here again to get the mother rattle. Agnes needs it. You must have it—don't you?" I ended on what must have been a forlorn note.

"Don't cry, baby. I don't have Agnes' rattle. Tell her I said she must be getting senile."

I stuttered something in agreement. Ruby turned on her booted heels and went inside the cabin, slamming the door. I was furious. Agnes had sent me on a wild goose chase.

And Ruby—that crazy Ruby. I sat down on the porch, wanting desperately to rest and have a cup of tea. Ruby could have been a little more hospitable.

Rolling thunderheads were gathering in the sky. The sun shone from the cloudy depths. Arrows of brilliant gold shot out from the light-edged clouds.

"Goodbye, Ruby," I called to the closed door.

Paint and I set off at a good pace. Her coat had not even turned with perspiration, except in the crease of her shoulders—she was in excellent condition. There was rain in the air, and a light mist was forming around the valley floor, where it came up to meet the high rocks. I was riding into the wind, and Paint's mane was picking up in the strong breeze and flying in my face. I was anxious to get home. I kept watching the sky for a storm, but the clouds began to dissipate, revealing the sun again. I watched a red-tailed hawk circle in an air draft. We stopped by the stream, and Paint drank until I pulled her head up and urged her on. I was still fuming about the mother rattle.

It was early evening when I arrived at the south pasture. I dismounted, wishing I had a carrot for Paint. I put my arms around her neck and scratched behind her ears, and she lay down and rolled in the green grass, scratching her back, much as I had done earlier with Agnes.

"See you soon, Paint," I said, waving.

I headed off for the cabin. I was famished, and I wanted a good explanation of why I had to go all the way to Ruby's when she didn't have the rattle. I heard the flute, caught sight of the porch, and noticed three people sitting there. My jaw fell open. Ruby was sitting with Agnes and July. How had Ruby gotten there before me?

Coming up, I stammered, "Ruby, you beat me."

"I took a short cut." She was laughing at my astonished expression.

I glanced up at the treetops, trying to calm myself. I carefully sat down on the porch step.

"You couldn't have gotten here before me," I said. "I rode due east."

"As you see, I'm here. Did you get lost?"

Agnes laughed. I glared at her. "Ruby said you have the mother rattle."

Agnes snapped her fingers as if she suddenly remembered. "Oh, that's right. I forgot."

"You purposely sent me on a wild goose chase for that rattle," I said accusingly. I was really mad.

"Wild goose chase," said Ruby, flapping her elbows like wings and sticking her neck out exactly like an angry goose. "Honk, honk! Wild goose chase!" She ran around the porch, honking and flapping. Agnes gave her a furious look of disdain.

"Cut it out, Ruby," Agnes said.

"Then give me back my rattle. The mother rattle is my rattle."

"Ruby," Agnes said, stamping her foot. "You know perfectly

well the mother rattle is mine. You gave it to me four years ago."

"No, I didn't either. I loaned it to you. There's a big difference."

"You gave it to me," Agnes said emphatically.

"Agnes, you must be losing your mind. I would never give you my rattle. Now give it back."

"I will not. It's mine," said Agnes.

I sat there on the step in disbelief. July's playing was softer, the same blank eyes staring into the distance.

"No, the mother rattle is mine," said Ruby. "I traded it with Cloud Woman."

"It's mine," shouted Agnes. "Isn't that so, Lynn?"

"Well, yes. That's what you told me," I said. "Keep me out of it."

"See, there's your proof," Agnes said, pointing at me.

"Oh, taking her side," Ruby said. "That's it. Everyone is against me."

"I'm not taking anyone's side, Ruby," I said. "Why can't you both sit down and discuss this in an adult way?"

"What do you mean, like this?" Ruby sat down with her nose stuck in the air, her head cocked coyly. Agnes sat opposite her with her hands clasped in a ladylike fashion. Both women's faces were prim, and their lips pursed.

"Now then, let's discuss my rattle," said Ruby.

"My, my, Ruby dear. You're mistaken there. It's a bit of a bother when you're so dreadfully mistaken."

"Now ladies," I said very seriously. "Where did the rattle in question first come from?"

Agnes and Ruby could stand the charade no longer. They put their arms around each other and giggled like children. They were holding their sides and jumping up and down. I realized I had been tricked again. The whole thing was a complete hoax.

I left them in disgust and went inside the cabin for something to eat, then came back out and sat down. Agnes and Ruby were still clowning around. Ruby was smoking a cigarette. She rolled it around in her fingers, blew a stream of smoke, threw it down, stamped it out, and lit another. She was chain-smoking.

Later, well along into the evening, the faces of Agnes and Ruby became suddenly serious.

"It's near twilight," Agnes said, handing me a mackinaw. She took her night-eagle rattle, and Ruby carried her turtle-shell mother rattle. As we went outside again, the sky was pink and gold and flaming orange.

We walked around past the right of the cabin, through a big crack in the rocks that I hadn't known was there, and down a narrow, treacherous path that fell away to a sheer drop. I clung to the rock face and watched my step. Then we passed through a shallow crease in the rocks into a gulley with boulders strewn around like giant agates striped orange and crimson in the sunset. The gulley took us down to a narrow granite ledge clinging to the cliff. I noticed the marks of tools, a carving of an animal, and an indistinguishable face above. Finally we worked our way down into a round area within the rocks about twenty or thirty feet across, with a shallow cave at one end. There were the remains of several fires, and new wood was piled at the back of the cave.

"Lynn, you place the wood for the fire," Agnes directed.

Agnes showed me how to place kindling and stack the larger pieces, and they watched me as I fumbled around. At length, Ruby lit the kindling, and the fire was soon going.

"Look at the sky," I exclaimed. The sunset was now deep crimson and pink in all four directions. The pinnacles of rock and scrub cedar growing in the crevices were a play of flame-red shadows and black silhouettes. There was a pressure in my ears as if we'd dropped hundreds of feet. Agnes took my shoulders and pointed me toward the now dying twilight.

"This is the time when the world changes," she said. "The time when you can be transformed." The old women began shaking the rattles, singing, and shuffling back and forth around me.

"You are the center fire," Agnes said. She came up next to me, shook the rattle in my ear, circled my head round and round with it, and then backed further away.

"You are the flowering tree," Ruby said, her face grotesque in the new darkness. She shook the turtle rattle next to my other ear and round and round my head again, then stepped away, sounding like a snake poised to strike.

Both repeated these motions over and over again. The sky was black now, the fire yellow and crackling. Great swaying shadows played across the high rocks. The old women became dark tempests in the night, jumping and reaching with their rattles, circling me with the sound in the vaulted crater. I began to get dizzy. The sage smoke from the fire curved along the ground and swirled up around us, Agnes and Ruby moving in and out of the gray puffs, which smelled of cedar. The rattles were relentless. The darkness and smoke felt thick like my skin. The sound of the rattles was enormous and tangible, and I could taste their music. It was strong and powerful.

Agnes rose up in front of me with her night-eagle rattle, her glittering eyes tracking me. I was shivering. I felt like I was floating inside the rattle. The sound of it was deafening. My ears were pounding and I wanted to scream. Suddenly, I became the sound and could contain it no longer. It was as if a dam had burst, a dam of song and beat. I exploded into a red nothingness reflected into the hot glow around the rocks. It was as if my skull had cracked. Agnes' rattle had pulled me out of myself. The awareness of my physical being had disappeared. I looked down on the two women, and then I was them.

I soared for a moment, then the sound of Ruby's mother rattle pulled on me like a hand gripping my womb. Its incessant beat pulled me back into another kind of consciousness. The sound was almost hisslike. The singing of Agnes and Ruby now seemed very strange, far away. My mouth was dry. Pink sparks seemed to dart off me into the air, I felt warm, and my awareness centered around my stomach. Agnes and Ruby vanished, and countless babies started crying. All the babies in the world were gathered around me and in me, and I was an enormous bubble holding them all. I was lying on the ground.

"Those are dead babies that haven't been born yet," Ruby said, placing her hand on my belly. "They're inside you, always crying.

They have been crying for a thousand years, where the wheels of darkness spin forever."

I tried to sit up. Agnes wrapped a blanket around me.

"Take the trust of those crying children," she said. "Feel the power in yourself of woman, of mother. You are the very mother earth itself."

Tears were running down my cheeks. I felt cleansed, filled with new strength, and deeply happy. Ruby put out the fire. Agnes helped me to my feet, and we started to walk back up the trail.

The sky warriors smiled when a high warrior stole power.

—Agnes Whistling Elk

I heard the crow tapping at the window, then Agnes opened it to
let him in. It was a pleasant way to wake up. I opened my eyes to
see the tops of the shadowy green hills and the hanging clouds
floating above. Crow was fluffing his feathers on the table, sleepily
blinking his eyes, and shivering. The coffee smelled wonderful.

"Where are Ruby and July?" I asked, sitting down to breakfast.

"They went for a walk," Agnes said. "They will be gone most of
the day." She shrugged. "At least now we don't have to listen to
that racket. That flute hurts my ears."

I smiled and nodded in agreement. "Agnes, tell me what
happened to me. I can scarcely believe what I'm remembering."

"You were brought between the rattles last night, the mother
rattle and the night-eagle rattle, two irresistible forces. Your life
was spun like a web between them. In a moment, they could have
torn you apart, but it was from them that you drew your power.
There is no part of you that is not of this mother planet. The
mother bear dances with the white-plumed arrows, and last night,
the points of the arrows met. The mother earth mingled her energy
with yours."

"I feel so much stronger."

"You are. The earth is a reservoir of energy. You merged with
that elemental force, and you are that force." She tossed a crumb
of fried bread to Crow, who hopped over and ate it quickly.

"I feel almost pregnant. Those babies—are they still inside me?"

"They have always been within you and within all women. Remember, everything must be born of woman. It is a power the world has forgotten. Men are interlopers. Many people, including some of my people, do not understand and would be angry for my words. Nevertheless, it is law. Woman is the flowering tree. You are the center of the universe, of creation, the mother earth. You needed to relearn this and build up your strength. Now your training can begin."

I was exuberant. "Training to steal the marriage basket?"

"Yes, so far I have fortified your body and your will. You are weak in many ways. You have many foolish attachments. I have to shake you free of them so I can lead you to power. We will begin with a history lesson—one that's not in the textbooks. I want you to take notes."

Agnes sounded so professorial I laughed.

"I'm quite serious, Lynn. I want you to remember this. Write it all down. Your journal and pencils are in the top dresser drawer."

I got them. I felt like a schoolgirl, poised and ready to write. Agnes picked up a long stick and pointed.

"Look in that direction," Agnes said. "And never tell anyone the direction you are looking. It is as sacred as your true name. Long ago, the sacred grandparents said that there was no day and no sun. The Great Spirit was the only. The Great Spirit was the center. The Great Spirit was the source without end. The grandparents told the daughter winds to blow the macrocosm into existence. The Great Spirit hid and divided up into niece and nephew. Together they sang the creation song. Everything vibrates with this voice—the universe, the galaxies, the sun and the earth. Light and darkness and all things are but a song of the Great Spirit. The Great Spirit is sleeping in all the named and nameless things.

"Many and all things happened as the grandparents foretold. What is forever but a breath to the Great Spirit? The design of the universe is nothing. All of time is but the snap of an arrow in the bow of the Great Spirit. The song of the tribes of plants was sung. The song of the animals was sung. The song of the tribes of man was sung. Every world was remembered in song and no world was forgotten. The Great Spirit is sleeping in all the named and nameless things.

"The Great Spirit chose this circle. The Great Spirit lifted up both palms, sang sweetly, and made seven bubbles. The bubble we are in is in the middle. The wheel has turned many times, and there have been many migrations. All the land has shifted, but the backbone of mother earth has remained. If the two-leggeds break her backbone, she will wobble off and die. That is the limit, which even her body cannot stand.

"I have spoken with the shaman tree, the remembering tree. First there was the sun. Second—the earth. Third—plants. The tree looked up and was lonely. 'I want many children,' the tree said. The moon lodge of the tree spoke it to the sun lodge of the tree and the sun lodge spoke it into being. The humans, the two-leggeds, walked the many wolf roads. The humans painted many laws.

"It was at any point on the circle of forever. Some call it the beginning, some call it the end." Agnes pointed again with her stick. "Down there was an island country the Indians called the Land of Six-Fingereds. I call it the Country of Thieves. Everyone prospered, because everyone had many blankets and provisions. No one needed anything, because everything was there. Everyone had plenty. Everyone was happy and blessed by the mother sea. The weather down there was hot—I mean really blistering hot. Heat shimmered over the island country in waves. You would think that beings who lived in an island country like that would be slow and witless. Not so. They were very nervous and quick beings. They were always running around the island.

"All things have laws. The law on the island was to play and have fun. So that is why the beings were moving about and doing something—stealing and thieving, whatever they could get their hands on. Remember, if you lived on the island, you were raised to be a thief. You were nurtured and trained from the time you were born. Beings who didn't steal were considered crazy, but that was okay too.

"Besides stealing, the island beings were liars. You had to piece together the truth from lies. If an island being ever told you the truth, it was either by accident or else it was done to confuse you. It sounds complicated, but this island country had very advanced ways of doing things most of the time. Nothing was known of murder or anything like that. Maybe the country of thieves sounds like a bad place, but it was pretty good. No one was ever bored. It all worked for those beings, and they had good simple hearts. It was wonderful to lie, cheat, and steal if it was done purely and properly and no one got hurt. When they caught a thief, they laughed. When island beings saw something they wanted, they took it—obeying the law. That was law. You could steal anything from anyone at any time.

"So, these island beings developed patience and skill. They were good at lying low and blending into the background until the right moment to rob something. They were the first invisible ones, and they knew the laugh of the invisible. There is invisibility in laughter. They could forget themselves and make others forget, too. They could conform to their surroundings so well you couldn't see them. In this bush country, there are so many things for your eyes to learn to see. So many things are invisible. So many things are not what you think they are. The whole bush would transform if you knew how to see it. But even with the best of bush vision, you couldn't see an island being. Such masters of the art of thieving haven't been seen since those ancient days.

"There are ways to reach the six-fingereds. Eat something. It is brown with a large cap that looks like a wide tipi. Men have eaten the legs off the bottom, uprooted the sacred food, for nothing. They only find the jade-eyed cat. Only a tall man or woman with his head above the earth can eat the medicine of knowing. Yet don't be deceived by the mushroom—that was the mistake of the island. The mushroom was too tall for them. They had to spit it out, and that made the earth rumble and caused the end. It was their error.

"The delights of the Country of Thieves went on through many long seasons, but then the island split in half. Hot whirlwinds rose up without regard to anything. The whole island rolled and thrashed and boiled and then submerged into the sea, killing everyone. It never surfaced again, and the wisdom of the race was nearly lost.

"Tobacco would have taught them—they would have seen water bows. It will happen again. Men know nothing of the steps to the altar, but my people know exactly what happened even though now there are those who say we wanted blood. Our altars could speak of all things to come. Climb this sacred ladder, Lynn, and make tobacco offerings to the cat. Drum me your footsteps to the sacred mountain. Fall down on the bleeding earth and cry.

"If you wish to know about significant things, those island beings were not ready to die so their spirit remained. They died with the name of the Great Spirit on their lips. It was too late to spare them, but the island beings were guided up from the foaming lake. The spirit of those beings went together as one, a phosphorescent being whose hands have six fingers. He now walks the earth as the greatest thief. Sometime you can dream to him and have him put something of power in your medicine bundle. If you reach him, he can help you get the basket from Red Dog. Yes, it would be your great fortune to locate and attach yourself to the spirit of the Country of Thieves, and let that spirit guide you. That thief could be your greatest ally. If you see the great six-fingered one on a moonlit night, you want to sing for joy. Touch the earth with both hands and pat your stomach with its blessing."

Agnes paused a moment, and I asked her if the story was true. Emphatically, she said it was. I asked her about the mushroom, and she said that she might tell me more about it one day.

"Right now, Lynn," Agnes said, "you should try to remember the six-fingered being in case you meet him. That was the purpose of the story but now you need to know about my people," she continued. "That is another reason I told you about the six-fingereds. You see that there have been many worlds. Not so long ago, it was altogether different. Everybody did the same thing.

There was quilling, beading, and tanning hides. Some humans made pipes. Some made shields. There were great hunters and great warriors. There were great healers. But we all did practically the same thing. Can you see that?"

"Yes, I think so," I said. I was writing furiously.

"The only difference at that time was how we did it. Some humans could do things better than others, but no one liked to do the same thing over and over. When the spirit of the doing was captured, we left it at that. We told a good story and we left it at that. We chanted a good chant and left it like that. We sang a good song and let in return. There was an exception—when a thing had power, we kept it. We kept the knowledge.

"The camp was not divided. Women had as much power as men. As I have told you, women are the source of all power. There were very great women chiefs, and women were high warriors as well as men.

"Let's pretend that you were a high warrior, Lynn, in those times. Everyone recognized a high warrior. Everyone talked about you. They said Lynn did thus and so, Lynn counted coup on so and so, Lynn stole so and so from so and so. Your deeds and your honor were well known. All the high warriors knew each other. There were many laws involved in being a high warrior." Agnes smiled mirthfully. "Imagine it now. You're a high warrior in those days.

"It is best to remember some things. This was before the horse. There were vast distances around here—hundreds and thousands of miles. It was a long walk, a hundred miles, to the next camp. You got pretty tired. Even with a horse, that's a long ride.

"Imagine yourself walking into an enemy camp to count coup on Ben and Drum. It wouldn't be any fun for them to fight you when you were tired. What kind of honor would there be in it for them? They would want you to be at your best, a high warrior, so they would have honor. And remember, too, that every young warrior wanted to count coup on a high warrior. What happened was that the camp put you up in what was called the enemy tipi. They fed you the best food and gave you the finest of everything.

The whole camp got excited and came out to see Lynn, the great warrioress. I think this took the place of TV and radio back there.

"The next day you went out to fight Drum. You had on your best clothes. Your knife and your ax were sharpened. The whole camp was watching. The idea was not to kill Drum, not hurt or scalp him, but to humiliate him. Cut his braids or make everyone see him as a coward. You get in the big fight with Drum. Everyone sees that you are the better warrior. They see you can take his braids, but you don't even do that. You cut his breeches and you cut a tuft of pubic hair. Everyone laughs uproariously. You turn and offer your back so Drum can kill you, but you know he won't. He would never be a great warrior if he did. No human would ever respect him again. In a day or two, you fight Ben or any other warrior who challenges you. All the time, you stay in the enemy tipi and are treated with honor and respect.

"That was warring.

"It is important that you know about stealing. Stealing is a sister art to sorcery, and all true sorcerers know how to steal power. Power can either be entrusted to you or stolen by you, but in either case, you have to know how to keep it. There are certain powers that a sorcerer dies with, that seep back into the mother earth and return to their source. There are spots hidden around the world where the great chiefs danced for power, and the spirit of those dead warriors resides there. If you can find one of these spots and conquer the spirit, you can have his strength and he is greatly honored. To do that, you must be a great warrioress. Somewhere on mother earth are the places where great men like Buddha, Christ, and Crazy Horse found their power. If you are given power, you must know how to keep it. If you steal power, you probably will not have as much trouble keeping it. If you stumble on power and don't take it because of lack of courage, you are not worthy of being a sorcerer. You see why you must first have a courageous heart before you can take power?

"First on the list for a high warrior to steal was a woman or a man. It didn't make any difference. It was an honor for a woman or a man to be stolen by a high warrior. Many marriages happened in this way. Remember now, back in the days I'm speaking of, it was forbidden to marry someone from your own camp.

"Next in the order of importance of things to steal were shields, staffs, big arrows or lances, bows, and so forth. If a high warrior could steal these objects, it was very good. But now, I must speak of greater gain.

"You can see there were many roads to power. Power is gained primarily from visions and dreams, but now I hope it makes sense to you that it was also honorable to steal power. To do that, you wanted to steal the great medicine shields, power objects, and medicine things, the things of power. But even then, these objects did you no good unless you knew how to use them. Mishandled, they could kill or injure you. It was a very great risk. To steal power was the most dangerous, because if you stole one of these power objects, it was the duty of the keeper to kill you. There were even more dangerous things to steal. If you could sneak up and steal a power song or ritual, then it was the duty of the whole camp to kill you.

"Stealing was one method for a high warrior to excel and become a medicine person. The sky warriors smiled when a high warrior stole power.

"Pretend that you have to confront me for power. Pretend for a moment that you are more powerful than I am and that you can remember me in other lives the way Drum tried to kill you. You can steal all my medicine in a blow from your medicine power. What do I do? I am an old woman, but that's no excuse. You are stronger than I am, and I know it. I am honored. I cry and beg the Great Spirit to take care of you and give you even more power. You have come from the enemy lodge and I am honored. A medicine woman is always honored by the successor. Teachers want their knowledge to be stolen. That's the way it used to be. And that's the way it still is. The old way is still with the ones of knowledge. But now, nothing is the way it looks.

"That old way was a good way, a sweet way. Then everything in the world changed abruptly. It is said that a man came to a Dakota village, the first white man anyone ever saw, and everyone was curious. They weren't sure what he was, if he was a man or what. The medicine men came and looked at him, then the chiefs. A medicine man shook his head and said, 'Maybe this man, if he is a man and not some spirit, ate too much chalk.'

"The white man tried to tell everyone his stomach was about to touch his backbone—he was hungry. But since no one understood his language and he didn't know how to sign, it was too bad for him.

"The chiefs said, 'If he is a man, he must have some strange sickness, and maybe it will spread. I don't want to turn color and look like him. He is going to die—we should kill him. And if he is not a two-legged, and has taken this form for some reason or another, it won't hurt to kill him.'

"Either way, killing him was thought to be the merciful act.

"By this time, some women who had come up to look at the white man asked, 'Can't you see? He's just a man like anyone else. He will starve to death unless he gets something to eat. Give him a knife and let him cut some meat away from those deer carcasses.'

"In those days, I have to tell you, fat was very scarce. Fat was the most valued and important part of any animal. If a human didn't get enough of it, he would die quickly, and there weren't many places to get it. Fat was precious.

"That woman gave the white man a knife and pointed to the deer that were hanging nearby. The man rushed up and cut the fat away from every deer and ate it. That was the first white man we ever saw, and those Dakota called him wasichu, which means takes-the-fat.

"The medicine people looked at that white man with the deer oil running down his face, then looked at one another. They knew it was all over, and they were right. The long knives came and took much more than deer fat. It all ended after that, and today you have this larger world hoop—the hoop of many nations.

"Medicine remained, but it came to be hidden. True knowledge, though, has always been hidden, given only to those who are worthy of it. It has to be that way. There are many secrets, and many of them are coming to light in your time. Red Dog is master of all those lost arts. He knows how to keep power, and how to steal it in the first place. He took the marriage basket, didn't he? He says 'Who will dare face me? Who will defeat me? Who has power enough to steal from me?' In your world, all the big thieving is done on paper. Yes, write it all down. Maybe you should write a book about Red Dog. That would get him. He wouldn't like that—he likes to remain disguised. Learn how to see him. You have taken too many things for granted. Your vision is but a glimpse. Everything is disguised.

"What is a medicine woman? We are travelers of the dimensions. Do not be caught in the prisms of eternity. Start thinking with your stomach. There are two dogs who stand guard in your stomach. Their names in English are jealousy and fear. One guardian dog is jealously fearful, the other fearfully jealous. They are medicine to protect you.

"Continue to use your intuition—you can never solve a problem on the level at which it is born. To steal the marriage basket you have to be relentless in your pursuit. Be the master of your destiny, because you have the necessity to manifest yourself.

"You are now walking into the sacred mountains where the bear dances with the white-plumed arrows. You have heard the dreamers. Emotions are born the moment you are connected to something, and you are connected to the dreamers. Follow the right trail and become one thing. Become a woman. In your world, womanhood is lost."

Agnes quit talking. I finished writing and drained the last of my tea. I didn't know what to say. Agnes left the cabin, and the warm sunshine streamed inside. I heard birds singing.

Agnes opened the door. "Put your notes away and follow me," she said.

Outside, we walked quickly up the trail and turned to the left, into a meadow blooming with yellow flowers. Bees and grasshoppers were skipping over the plants, and the broad glare of the sun was warm and wonderful. Before returning to the cabin, Agnes told me to spend the rest of the day in the field and not to feel separated from "what is seen." I walked through the fields until late afternoon.

It was almost dark when I heard Agnes calling me to eat. As soon as I heard her voice, I ran to the cabin, where the smell of the food was wonderful.

Agnes dished me up a bowl of hot soup with a strange, rich taste. The dusk was circling round us in gray shadows, encroaching upon the small flickering light of our candle. A soft wind blew through the open door. Agnes sat on the bed sewing on an old mackinaw. Without looking up at me, she asked, "Lynn, what do you really want?"

"What do you think I want? I want the marriage basket."

Agnes said nothing. I sipped the last drop of soup and put the spoon down. Agnes laid the mackinaw aside and looked at me directly.

"To get the marriage basket, you must become the proper receptacle," she said. "You must ripen your void so that the energy of what you want, in this case the basket, will flow magnetically toward your belly. You must become what she wants so that there is no separating you. When you think of yourself as a separate entity, you will obstruct that current and the basket will defeat you."

I was bewildered by these terms. "How will I know when I have ripened my void?"

"You will simply become aware of your power. You will feel your time. You cannot avoid it."

"Agnes, I don't understand your terminology. How can I learn all these things?"

"That's why you are here—to learn."

She put the mackinaw in her dresser drawer, walked out onto the porch, and sat down. I poured a cup of tea and followed. Agnes was watching the northern lights. Gold and pink, they seemed to be heralding a carnival on the other side of the world. I sat down on the steps and marveled at the play of color across this strange woman's face. I felt a special tenderness for her. Her face was a messenger of great pain to me, because it reminded me that what I had known as my life was dying. I couldn't even explain to myself how I was different, but I knew I was evolving into a person I wouldn't have recognized a few months ago. It was like being in love.

"Tonight, the grandparents have a vital gift for you. I'm going to give you your medicine." Agnes patted the wooden boards and motioned me to sit closer to her. "If you were an animal, what would you be?"

I was puzzled. "You are always asking me questions that I have a hard time answering." I thought for several minutes and then said, "I've always loved horses, or maybe a deer?"

Agnes smiled at me. "You are a black wolf."

She watched my reaction and then put out a hand and touched my forehead. "Waken within yourself." She took her finger away. The touch gave me a peculiar sensation throughout my body. "You are the black wolf instead of the white wolf, because you wear the black cloak of contemplation. If you were the white wolf, you would be more outward, more extroverted. You track through the forests for what you want and then come back to the pack and curl up in the sun and think about it. You're a lone wolf who is afraid of being alone. Let me tell you a story.

"In the beginning when the world was formed, the chiefs sent the wolf cubs out to explore and measure the world. They went down all the trails of the world and said, 'This is the way it is and that's the way it was.' Wolf medicine means measure. Wolves are good mathematicians if they want to be. If you are one with your medicine you can never be tricked, because you've been down all the trails. It's a very powerful and hypnotic medicine.

"I'll give you an example. The wolf goes down to the river in the early morning. He sees his breakfast swimming out there and dances playfully along the bank. All the geese are intrigued and mesmerized. They swim toward the dancing wolf. When the geese are close enough, he jumps into the water and kills as many geese as he needs—his can be a very dangerous medicine. A hunter would be very lucky to kill or trap even one wolf, and that's because the wolf teaches the other wolves what the hunters are up to. And if you were the hunter, it would be impossible. You cannot kill your own medicine. If you did you'd be in very big trouble.

"The wolves set up the first school. They were the first teachers. The wolf lives in a way that makes his pack strong. He always provides food for the aged and sick, trains the pups, and defends his territory against other wolves. He tracks like no other animal. He has stamina, and he can go without food for great periods of time. The wolf is big medicine, and you must remember I didn't choose the wolf for you. You are wolf."

Agnes sat back.

"I'm beginning to see. You've touched something deep inside me," I said. "I do feel sort of like a wolf. I love to discover new trails, and I feel at the center of my being a new kind of awareness. Hyemeyohsts Storm must have known my medicine, because he gave me a piece of wolf fur. What is the purpose of having medicine?"

I leaned back against the post, amazed at how wolflike I was feeling.

"The purpose of medicine is power. You go to a psychiatrist and he tells you your head is fouled up. What he's doing is helping you to introspect and learn about your own character. But since native people have observed the four-leggeds and winged ones and all the forces of nature for thousands of years, we know your closest kinship. When I tell you you're the black wolf, you look within yourself and you know that you truly are. When you understand the powers of the black wolf, you too will have those powers. All the medicines are good and have power. White people have this thing that says, 'I'm not a snake. I'm not a squirrel. I'm something important.' They separate, and that's their tragedy."

For a moment Agnes stared at me, her eyes holding the swiftly moving hues of the northern lights. My mind was filled with this new information. I took the wolf fur out of my pocket and felt its softness. Agnes got up abruptly, and we went inside the cabin without saying anything further.

"Clean up the cabin," Agnes said. "Ruby and July will be here soon. We are all going to take a sweat together in the sweat lodge down by the stream. There is much to learn, and many meanings to this experience you are bound for."

"What is the reason for the sweat lodge?" I asked, feeling nervous.

"I'll get to that in a moment—it is very involved. The purpose of a sweat is to purify the spirit and body to facilitate communication with the Great Spirit. Tonight, I want you to listen for your medicine—your black wolf self. Through this purification you will find guidance and revitalization."

Agnes spoke to me at length about the meaning of the sweat lodge.

"We must move quickly," she said, "if you are the one who dares steal the basket from Red Dog. Tonight, after your spirit has been cleansed, I will paint your body in a certain way, and we will dance your dance to the spirit world. You will transform and become one with your medicine, and you will know the power of it. You will dance in a spot that will become charged with your wolf energy. It will be one of your places of power. Think of these things and then, if you truly want power, all you can do is submit to it."

We went outside, and the northern lights blazed up in a fiery gale, orange, green and blue-white. Far in the distance, I could hear the strains of the flute. Moments later, I saw the dark forms of the old woman and the girl loom up in the darkness.

"I almost forgot about the sweat," Ruby said. "But here we are." She didn't seem tired from her long trek. I felt a prickly uneasiness standing near her.

Agnes gathered us together like a mother hen and urged us down the trail toward Dead Man's Creek. I carried my old towel from the car. The air was perfumed with the moist, dense clamor of growth.

Ruby and Agnes were giggling up ahead. July, as surefooted as Paint, tooted along behind. I caught sight of a mound in the distance, one I hadn't seen before. When July and I arrived at it, Agnes told me to sit down and be silent.

"Just watch us build the fire and heat the rocks. Think of it as the eternal fire. It is built in a sacred manner, and by that fire we shall be made pure and come closer to the source of all power. Sit in a sacred way and dream." Agnes left me sitting in the dirt by the creek.

I saw that Ruby had put July's flute by Agnes' pipe bag. July was docile and quiet, to my amazement. We sat side by side in a forest clearing. The northern lights were tamer, and the stars were massive dots of brilliant ice blue in the black. It seemed even darker, now that the fire crackled. Huge yellow and orange flames leapt up into the night, and the air was close and heavy. Agnes sat near the fire, her face bathed in orange, and began to beat softly on her drum and chant. She chanted for a long time, then began to pray over the fire.

After a few minutes, Ruby said "Ho!" Agnes walked to the earth mound and placed her full tobacco pipe on the earth. Under her direction, July and I took off our clothes and entered the lodge, bowing low because the entrance was only four feet high. Inside, I gave a silent prayer to the Great Spirit. Agnes prayed aloud, and we moved around in the direction of the sun. Then I sat by the door, opposite Agnes. We all remained silent for a while. The air was pungent with sage.

Earlier Agnes had told me never to be petty, to think of the highest, and to remember the goodness of all things. I tried to do these things as we sat in the darkness, the only light coming from the doorway. The fire leapt and crackled outside—Ruby was tending a real bonfire. She handed the pipe in to me and I placed it in front of me as Agnes had instructed, the stem pointing west. Then, using a large forked stick, Ruby slid a glowing rock to the center of the sweat lodge, into the dugout altar. My knees nearly touched it.

Ruby said something in Cree.

Agnes directed me to touch the rock with the foot of the pipe, and then we all gave thanks in Cree.

Ruby guided in more rocks, one for each direction, one for the earth, one for the sky. Agnes told me to offer the pipe to the sky, the earth, and the four directions, and then to light it. After taking a few puffs and rubbing smoke all over my body, I handed the pipe to July on my left. She took it and puffed. Agnes puffed, passed it back to me, and told me to purify it and carefully empty the ashes onto the edge of the sacred altar. Then she told me to pass the pipe back around to her. She held the pipe above the altar, stem pointing west, then moved it along the sacred path to the east where Ruby, standing just outside the doorway, took it.

The rocks in the center were glowing a fiery red. The lodge was small, maybe eight feet across, a basketlike womb of bent willows covered with various hides. Suddenly, Ruby closed the flaps and placed a trade blanket over the entranceway. We were immersed in a darkness that Agnes had told me represented the darkness of the soul, the ignorance from which we must purify ourselves so that we may have light.

I heard Agnes' voice in the darkness. "During the ceremony, the flaps will be opened four times to remind us that we have received the light during the four ages." She began a long prayer to the spirits in Cree. "Lightning underground, the moles," she said. Then she sprinkled water on the rock four times from a wooden cup with her eagle fan, all the while praying to the grandparents.

The fragrant steam hissed and coiled upward. It was becoming incredibly hot, and I was struck by the blackness—the chamber was dense, dark, and thick. Then Agnes called the Whiskey Jack, or Bright Morning Star Sky, and sprinkled water four more times. I put my head between my knees to breathe better. Then she called rainbows, then the eagles, and sang a beseeching, melodious song. She was very emotional. I started to cry. I thought the heat would reach a certain level and then stop, but it kept building and intensifying almost beyond endurance. The glowing rocks were like the glittering eyes of middle earth itself. Agnes called for her changing powers—the deer—and sprinkled water four more times. I realized I was praying out loud. Rivulets of sweat poured off my scalp and down into my eyes. I blended with the intense heat.

Ruby threw back the blanket and flaps, and a rush of cool air enveloped us. The light from the fire threw eerie shadows around our dark pocket of sacred prayer. I was disoriented by the sudden light but thankful for breathing. Agnes passed around a cup of water and we all rubbed it on our bodies. I felt humble and grateful.

The flap was closed again, and I became aware of July, rocking back and forth, moaning quietly. Then she began to sob desperately. I began to wonder about the pain in the world. I didn't know if tears were rolling down my cheeks, or sweat—I could hardly breathe. I was immersed in a black hole of sadness and abandonment. A shimmering haze lifted and spread in the enclosure.

"Lynn," Agnes said, "you have come to me as a rainbow warrioress. You are a bridge between the Indian world and the white world, a bridge on this great Turtle Island. When you know yourself you will know your way. When you know your way you will know authority. When you know authority you will see the spirit. When you see the spirit you will see the people."

Next she instructed me to call for the wolf, my medicine. Then she said, "I am teaching you your song. Listen to it and sing it with me."

As I sang, eyes closed, a green and blue wheel appeared behind my lids, turning first to the right, then to the left, and hypnotized me. I had a vision. I was outside the lodge, and standing before me was an old woman with a little girl.

"How did you get here?" I asked. "And who are you?"

"All trails lead back to the center—all spirit." The vision disappeared, and I was back in the sweat lodge.

I heard Agnes asking, "What did you see? Where were you?"

I told her.

"That was Wolf Girl and her grandmother," Agnes said. "What did they say?"

I told her.

"Yes, all ways, all religions, lead back to the center. Walk within goodness."

"But I don't understand who the old lady and the little girl were."

"They are wolf medicine."

"What does that mean?"

"Let's answer this way, my daughter. Love is a good guide. Knowledge is a good guide. Sharing is a good guide. Self-teaching is a good guide. I do not have to believe to know sorrow—I know when I sorrow. I don't have to believe to know love—I know when I love. I don't have to believe to have joy—I know when I am joyful. To be here I am here. So do not believe that you are only human. Know yourself. There are many medicines."

"Your words are making me feel good, Agnes, but they are not all connecting in my mind."

"You had a child once."

"Yes."

"You didn't have it in your mind to have a child. You had your baby girl within your whole being—not just your mind. Let it be born."

I felt a pang of helplessness, as if ropes wrapped around me were strangling my slightest movement. I wanted to scream and run, to get out of the torturing heat and confinement. I willed myself into submission, but then, miraculously, the darkness began to breathe with me. The glow of the rocks began to pulsate with my pounding heart. My body seemed to be melting, and my hands were fisted in a strange way. I tried to pull my fingers apart but they bent oddly, like claws, and I could not move them. I was hunched over, my head cocked sideways, and when I blinked my eyes in the fragrant gloom, my face felt frozen. My lips curled up and outward to expose my teeth. I was snarling—all barriers were gone. I felt the soft black hair on my underbelly. I was the primal she-wolf, my head thrown back, howling mutely.

Agnes spoke softly in Cree. I couldn't understand her words, but I knew they were to reassure me.

The flap opened and closed again. I was totally possessed of the she-wolf spirit, with no sensation except wolf sensations. I crouched over my pups, who whined and whimpered in the dark lair-labyrinth. I lost all sense of what happened next, but at some time later I heard the rippling of the creekwater. Agnes was sitting beside me.

"You were blessed tonight, Lynn," she said. "Your wolfness is very powerful."

I started shivering with fright. "I couldn't uncurl my fingers, and then I was a real wolf."

"Don't worry. I am happy," Agnes said. "The dreamers were right. You are the perfect huntress to steal the basket."

I revived slowly. My hair was wet and clung to my head, and Agnes put a wool blanket around my shoulders that smelled of cedar. The sound of the stream became distinct, louder. I started to get up, but Agnes stopped me.

"Stay here for a while."

Agnes joined Ruby by the fire, and joined her in beating the drum. I could see only their silhouettes in the darkness.

The sliver of new moon was over the hills now, its light bleeding softly across the sky. July was seated downstream, watching the moon's placid and silver reflection floating on the water. A night-blooming flower was scenting the air.

"Come," Agnes said, turning to me. "We will go eat at the cabin and then prepare you for your dance."

She started abruptly up the trail. I scrambled and followed, forgetting my exhaustion.

"What did you say, Agnes? My dance?"

Agnes dismissed me with a gruff "Yes," and I fell back to watch after July, who was playing the flute again.

After we ate something at the cabin, I lay down to rest, dimly aware of Ruby and Agnes leaving, my sleep cradled by swells of wind blowing in the trees. I dreamed I was captured in a giant marriage basket and couldn't get out. I slipped every time I tried to crawl up the side of the basket.

"Wake up, Lynn," Agnes said, shaking me awake. I was glad to be out of the dream.

"The basket! I was dreaming about it again."

"I knew you were dreaming about something. You looked pretty funny," Agnes said, grinning.

Ruby, too, was leaning over me with amused curiosity and smiling. I was unnerved—Ruby had never smiled at me. It was incredible—that smiling, withered face.

Agnes took my arm and pulled me outside. It must have been past midnight.

"This is a sacred night for you. Put yourself in that sacred way as I have taught you, and we will soon go to power. Listen to your cousins singing, and I will be back."

Agnes went in the cabin, leaving me standing there. The coyotes were howling somewhere off in the hills. July was asleep, but still seated with her back against a post. I noticed the tree forms swaying in the wind, sat down on the porch steps, and waited.

Agnes and Ruby came out a few minutes later. We walked for a good distance into a stand of scrub cedar, then made an abrupt right turn between two boulders that towered above our heads. The sound of gravel under our feet broke the quietness of the night. The narrow path wound through several more boulders, and I was feeling dizzy and disoriented. Agnes and Ruby were so close to me I could feel their breathing.

Very quickly, we came to a clearing with the smell of something different in the air. I realized it was sulphur, or something very like it, mixed with the rich aroma of cedar and sage. We turned a corner and came to a smouldering fire that had obviously been burning for some time. Ruby tended to it and made the flames leap.

As I looked around me, my vision seemed partially impaired. Agnes led me over to the fire, where she laid out a beautiful old Indian blanket with a black and red storm pattern. There was a spring with steam rising from it nearby.

"Take off all your clothes, Lynn, and sit by the fire on the blanket," Agnes said.

She left while I was undressing, then returned with two clay pots with sticks in them. Ruby was chanting behind me, Agnes prayed, and the drum sounded in a deep, continuous beat. Their voices lifted in a beautiful song in a mysterious language that carried deep into the woods. I wished I knew the meaning of their ancient language.

The coals glowed, and flames licked up with every subtle change in the wind. I felt the heat against my bare skin. The blanket felt coarse and tightly woven. Ruby and Agnes danced back and forth on either side of me, Agnes shaking the rattle in my ear when she drew near enough. I was elated, but still disoriented. Ruby went to the opposite side of the fire, and continued to beat the drum and chant softly.

Agnes sat down in front of me. After a long hesitation, she said, "We have brought you here to this sacred place. It is a hidden place. Here you will undergo a new birth, for you will be painted here and changed forever. By being painted, you will begin a new relationship with your wolf medicine, and you will undertake new responsibilities."

Agnes dipped her fingers into one of the clay pots. She touched the center of my head where my part was—it felt wet—and she drew a line down the center.

"This paint is red for woman," she said. "That red line unites you with the earth, where everything dwells and is fertile."

With sure movements, Agnes put two more slashes of red under my eyes. The paint was cold and had a flowery odor, and for a moment I thought it was burning.

"Great Spirit, it is your will that this young woman is here to be painted. Let her who sits upon the ancient sacred ground be birthed pure, as from your sweat lodge. As I paint her in this sacred manner, purify her once more. Separate this young woman from her pains of the past." Then she told me to stand up.

I jumped up quickly. Agnes painted my legs red to the knees. I was standing unselfconsciously, facing the fire, oblivious to everything but Agnes' actions. She painted wavy lines down my left arm, then did the same to my right. Then she walked around me four times.

"We have drawn death here on this night," Agnes said, again facing me. "This power stands here with us. We have killed so many things. You travel now on the sacred path—you have begun a new walk. I welcome the one who is watching us, the guardian of the far-away. These lines on your arms are the symbol of the rainbow, the bow of the dreamers."

I was perfectly calm, watching Agnes with my heart, my eyes closed. I had felt her touch profoundly at every stroke of paint. I opened my eyes, and saw tears rolling down her cheeks. She reached down, picked up a bundle of folded buckskin, lifted it with both hands, and extended it to me. Ruby's drum resonated in my chest, pushing at me as though it were a flat hand.

"Put this on," Agnes said. I took the folded buckskin. "It is a dress and moccasins. I wore them when I was a girl. You have new clothes tonight, because you are a new woman."

Carefully I put them on. The dress was resplendent, with glass beads that shone in the firelight like drops of gold. There were various symbols and designs woven in porcupine quills, and fringe hung down from the sleeves and hem. It fit me perfectly, as did the beaded moccasins.

"You are being trained in the heyoka arts," Agnes said, resting a hand on my shoulder. "These garments will help you in your learning.

"Feathers will be a sign of your apprenticeship," she continued.

I turned my face right and left so that she could braid two owl feathers into my hair. I was being drawn into a feminine tenderness, yielding and quiet. I was inside a fiery throbbing bubble, floating in space. I had forgotten the world.

"Sit down, Lynn. I will tell you of my own teacher. I was married once, long ago, and I had a daughter. Winters are sometimes hard in the north. One winter day, she wandered out of the cabin into the snow. She was very young, my daughter, four years old. The dogs we had were trained to be ferocious. The dogs got to my daughter before I could and killed her. We brought her in our cabin and put her between us all night. I had planned to give the dress you are now wearing to my daughter. Now I give it to you. My daughter had the name of Little Black Wolf Dancing. After she died, I used to look into the east where the sun is born, trying to give my daughter back to the mother earth. Maybe I have always kept the dress because I couldn't let her go—my beautiful Little Black Wolf Dancing. And then I have looked into the west, where the sun dies, but not ever have I been able to give away my sorrow, until this moment. As the earth is my mother, I am your mother. Now I have a new daughter. My family, my clan, shall receive you as their own. My little wolf cub can live again in you."

I couldn't hold back my tears. Agnes patted my arm and continued. "That was before I knew anything, and I thought medicine people weren't worth bothering with. My husband was killed in a lumbering accident soon after that—I think he had lost heart. My grief was terrible. That's when I went to a heyoka and she taught me everything. Power came to me and I got my name, which means 'one who knows secrets.'

"Before that, I didn't care about my life or what happened to me. I didn't realize it, but there is big medicine in that abandon. I had heard that the heyoka could answer any question, and I wanted someone to explain the reason for my great sorrow to me. The old sacred heyoka woman answered everything with a question. She acted as if she didn't understand anything until I caught on to the fact that she lived at the center of the sacred hoop and had power to change anything any way she wanted. I spent hours telling her about my dead daughter. When I was finished talking, and asked her why Little Black Wolf Dancing was dead, she asked me, 'Who wants to know who is dead?'

"That woman was my teacher. She gave me her medicine after many years, and then she went away and died happily. She was a woman who stood in all places and could see everything. I loved her once I got to know her, and much of her lives in me. I do not know what would have happened to me if she had not shown me my way. Because of her, I have a life of purpose."

Agnes' eyes met mine, and I cried until I was spent of grief. I stood up, and Agnes and I walked away from the fire. My new moccasins were snug, and I could feel just enough of the earth beneath my feet. Agnes was carrying the two rattles. She stopped, stamped with her foot several times, and suddenly leapt into the air and spun around. She started trotting in a circle around me, bent forward. I was mesmerized. Her gait was stiff-legged, like the gait of a wolf—exactly like a wolf. She carried her head so that her eyes snapped out at me—glinting and cunning like an animal's. She brushed her hip against me, then stood off to one side and howled. Something welled up in me and I uttered an answering howl. It had a wistful quality and seemed far away, and the sound was not human.

Then something snapped and tore within my chest. It may have been that the drumbeat stopped. I heard a panting.

"Breathe four times deeply for the four directions," Agnes commanded in a strange, growling voice. Throw back your head and place both fists against your chin. Don't look at me yet."

I did as she instructed.

Her voice was frightening. "Do it again and this time, crouch and dash your two arms back behind you, expelling your breath. Pull energy up from the earth as you breathe out. Steal that energy by stamping your right foot. Make no mistake. The wolves know this spot and you can, too. Dart your head left and right and then center. Good. Now go around to the west and whimper like a wolf. Start trotting."

I followed her directions as best I could. The beat of the drum sounded, and I could feel my toes spreading under my weight as I trotted and whimpered. We reversed to the east, and as I brushed my arm against my face felt fur on my cheek. My ears pricked forward. My eyes hungered for an imagined prey. We trotted fast and then slow—always steady—to the north and then to the south. At the crest of a hill, we stopped and bayed, but it wasn't Agnes with me. I saw only a wolf—a strange sister there in the velvet darkness.

The drum stopped, and the spell was broken. My fangs retracted, my paws withdrew, and Agnes seemed to change form, to rear up on hind legs and become herself again. My own body reemerged somehow. I could barely follow Agnes to the hot pool, where she pulled off my new dress and shoved me into the hot sulphur-water. The water was red with paint, as if bleeding with the forces of nature.

"Wash it off."

I washed, crawled out, and lay on the bank, numb as I looked up at the stars. Agnes threw the blanket on me. "Come," she said.

I carried my beautiful dress, and wore my moccasins, back to the cabin. When I crawled into my sleeping bag, it was almost dawn.

The purpose of medicine is power.

—Agnes Whistling Elk

"I want you to make a wolf doll," Agnes said the next day.

I was sitting at the table, sipping sage tea. "A wolf doll?" I asked. "Do you mean like a wolf fetish?"

"You can make it to be anything you want, as long as it's wolf and doll. You can make it out of clay, dead grass, wood chips, pieces of hide, or anything else. You can even whittle it if you want to."

"How big should it be?" I asked, rather excited about making my own fetish.

Agnes motioned big and little with her hands. "You can make it as big or as little as you like. It will help you in many ways. You must remember the dance for your medicine constantly. There are mother powers that you have become aware of, and certain powers now need your protection. Understanding came to you in the form of dreams—the dreamers dreamed you awake. Now, put those dreams and powers into a tangible form. You can use them, and they can tell you much. Design a wolf doll interpreter for bridging the worlds. When you are finished, show me your work."

Agnes turned away from me in dismissal. Thoughts of the Indian dolls I had collected and sold flashed through my mind, and I grabbed a knife and something for lunch, and walked off down the trail toward Paint. I was thinking about her long black tail. It was a misty, foggy day, a good day to give form to my dreams. I was walking quickly up the slope of a hill, the shadows of rocks and grasses looming around me. The trail to the south pasture was obscured by the moving, misting forms of trees no longer familiar. I heard wings rustling and beating in the overhanging branches.

I arrived at the fog-blanketed pasture and found Paint. Her hooves disappeared into the white puffs layering the ground.

I took some of her tail for the wolf doll, then wandered around in the fog for the rest of the day. I scratched around in the dirt and climbed the trees, looking for feathers, pieces of bark, pieces of fur, anything unusual and appropriate. I discovered a fairly soft piece of wood by Dead Man's Creek, one that vaguely suggested a wolf body on four legs. It was about six inches long, and at one end there was a howling face—once I finished carving it. I took bits of sage, fur, and other things I scrounged, and made a lightning bundle. I wrapped it onto the belly of the wolf. The horsehair served as the tail, and I carved symbols of the night eagle and the bear onto its back. I had found glue and a piece of broken mirror in Agnes' cabin, and I glued pieces of broken shell in the mouth for snarling teeth and two pieces of the mirror above for eyes. I crushed some red berries and rubbed the wolf with the juice, which looked like blood. The bird nails worked well as claws. As I whittled and glued and put power into the new wolf, it began to develop a fearful presence. I found myself singing a strange song as I worked—I had been singing it over and over before I realized it. It was a dream song for me.

My wolf-doll was finished by twilight. He was howling and fierce, but he had an odd birdlike quality as well. That meant he could fly between the worlds—that he was at home in both earth and sky. I don't know why I called him "he," but he seemed masculine—perhaps because he was ferocious and angular. I admired him for a while, cradled him in my arms, and strode back to Agnes' cabin.

"Let's have a look," Agnes said, before I had a chance to say anything. "Set it on the table."

I put the figure down, and it seemed to dominate the room.

Agnes walked around it, cocking her head, her eyes glowing mysteriously.

"What can you tell me about the person who made it?" she asked.

"I made it."

"What can you see and know if you hadn't made it? When I look at something like this, I know who did it. In this case, you did it, so it is a perfect mirror of your own perception."

"It's just a doll," I said.

"No, it's not just a doll. I see who made it. If I had never seen you before in my life, I would know that the person who made this was female. She is white and has a very limited knowledge of wolves and animal life. When you made this, you were showing me your true nature. You are a woman with many masks. You have no reason for pretense with me."

"I'm not pretending about anything," I objected.

"Yes, you are. You are pretending to respect me, because you want something I can give you. But you really think I wouldn't fit into your world in California."

"Agnes, really."

"Yes, that's what you really think of me. You wonder what all this is going to cost you. You wonder if I'm going to call you collect from the bus depot some day. You think you're too good for us here."

"Agnes, if you think that about me, why do you let me stay with you?"

"I don't think that about you. I know that about you. You hope I don't show up on your doorstep because you don't know how you could explain me to your friends. You think I couldn't handle your life of excitement and glamorous people, don't you?"

"Well, I guess I was wondering some of those things."

"You're afraid I might not be properly impressed, or know what represents what. You're ashamed of my clothes, my poverty, my manners, everything."

I winced. "Agnes, I don't think it's fair for you to say that about me."

"This wolf doll tells me all that I need to know. Are you afraid you will hurt my feelings if you tell me yourself? You need this wolf-thing to do it for you?"

"You're just guessing. You can't possibly see that much in it."

"You like good food. You like to collect for aesthetic reasons—that's an easy one. I can tell that in a blink. You have a sense of humor—that's easy, too. You like to live in an environment you consider beautiful. You can't wait to get back to what you think of as familiar land. You can't wait to get back to where you can buy things—comfort, food, services."

"What's wrong with that?"

"Nothing, but here you have to work for it."

"What else do you see in the wolf, Agnes?"

"Here's one for you. See how the leather is wrapped on his bundle?"

"Yes," I said. I looked at it closely.

"Can you tell me anything at all from that?"

"I'm not sure."

"The maker is right-handed, because it twines sunwise. The maker is also a perfectionist—the twine has been tied and retied many times. By the way, why did you cut the horsehair from the tail instead of the mane?"

I was amazed that Agnes knew that. "I don't know. It just seemed like the right place."

"I thought so," Agnes said, laughing. "You have the makings of a true heyoka."

I laughed too, but I didn't completely understand the humor.

Agnes continued. "That doll tells me something of your delusions, what you think is important and meaningful, and what you're willing to die for. You understand nothing of food or the killing of a good friend with dignity. It talks to me of your stance in the world. It tells me what you want and what you don't want. You don't see your death and you won't go to death in a full way—as a good daughter of the universe. The huntress never makes excuses to death.

"There are merely two choices in life," she continued. "You can die like a frightened whore, or you can live like a worthy huntress and die like one. When your eyes meet those of the greatest huntress, you can say 'I am ready. When the hunt was on, I was valiant. I stalked my prey and killed it appropriately. I was a good provider for my camp, I ate my kill, and I gave it away with respect. I acted on your behalf and represented you well. I realize that I have lived off you, and now I am your meat. We are in agreement. I am ready to go with you to hunt in the spirit world.' "

"You see me as a coward?" I asked.

"You are not a dangerous woman. You are like a clipped bird in some ways—beating your wings without purpose. I see a woman who needs much more will and courage—true courage. You are not at all as simple as you look. The saddest thing I see is that you like to think you're important. For me, I prefer being important to fooling myself."

"How do you become important?"

"Learn of your death."

"I don't understand. What does death have to do with being important?"

"Plenty. Accept your death and become dangerous. Get power."

"Wait a minute. I'm totally confused. Do you want me to die?"

Agnes laughed loudly. "That's funny," she scoffed. "I can't stop you from dying. Throw away your juggler eyes and see what's real. People can appear important to you because of one thing and another. You fear them because they seem to have power of some nature. But if you knew of your death, you would be able to see which of those people truly have power, and few people do. You can only be dangerous when you accept your death. Then you become dangerous in spite of anything. You must learn to see the awake ones. A dangerous woman can do anything because she will do anything. A powerful woman will do the unthinkable because the unthinkable belongs to her. Everything belongs to her, and anything is possible. She can track her vision and kill it by making it come true."

"What are you suggesting? Are you going to teach me about death so I can steal the marriage basket?"

"I am going to begin to teach you how to hunt so that when you do your questing, you'll stand a chance. You don't want to walk around aimlessly, without knowing what you're doing. You hunt for food to nurture yourself and share with others. If I am successful, you will be terribly dangerous."

"Why did you want me to make a wolf doll?"

"I wanted to make it clear to you that nothing stands without reason. Things made deliberately are accurate mirrors of those who make them. You can develop your awareness by examining anything closely. Looked at properly, an object will cry out to you. When you know enough, you will see much about a person by the way she picks up a glass or pencil. You can see a thousand things in action. You can know all about a hunter by the way he builds a fire, just as you can know about a bird by the way it builds its nest. When you look at an object, you can see how much of a center it has. A true power object has a center. You are drawn to these things, and you don't even know why."

"What does all this have to do with the marriage basket?"

"We have been talking a great deal directly and indirectly about stealing. You have learned that before you can steal effectively, you must be a warrioress. Do you see that?"

"I remember—yes."

"Before you can be an effective warrioress, you must become an expert huntress—the great warrioress was beforehand a great huntress."

"What do I have to know to be an effective huntress?"

Agnes laughed like a child. "So many things, and even then you can't know all. You see that being a huntress is very complicated. Listen, there are many creatures to hunt. You can hunt and trap a spirit if you know how. There are spirit traps you can make, and traps to catch water babies, and even then you have to know how to make them food. For the moment, spirits are hidden from you—you think they are born in your imagination. But the imagination can turn on you and kill you if you don't know how to look at it straight. If you hunt a rabbit, that's one thing. If you hunt a grizzly, that's an entirely different thing. The rabbit and the grizzly are two kinds of game. Don't ever think that the rabbit is harmless. I've found rabbits can easily kill a man. Fortunately, even the good hunters rarely see a rabbit like this. If you tried to kill that kind of rabbit, he would thump his hind feet, the world would disappear for you, and you would die. Nor is the grizzly a task for the foolish hunter. Never underestimate even the caribou. It is said that some caribou can scatter the mind to such distances, it will one day drive the hunter crazy. If it is meat you are hunting, you must never waste any of it—not even the bones. Hunted meat has a spirit. It has a big spirit that will make you strong. The sweet meat of the slave animals holds no responsibility to you. It tastes sweet, but it makes you fat and indolent. You have to be balanced in the physical world and balanced in the spirit world. Then those two balances have to again be balanced."

"And do you get that double balance by the food you eat?" I asked, trying desperately to follow Agnes' line of logic.

"Partially. If you eat slave meat, you don't think anyone can make you do anything. Those slave animals had traps around them, and so will you if you eat them. You can see a people by what they eat. A nation of slaves doesn't know anything about themselves or anyone else. There are so many kinds of food—food for the heart, food for the body, and food for your brain."

"Do you have to eat meat?"

"No. You try to eat medicine food, food with spirit. If you too are food, the chiefs of the plant and animal worlds will talk to you and tell you of your proper diets."

"Can you buy that kind of food in a grocery store?"

"Yes, most of the time; but you will have to know a lot more about awake food—for instance, which food suffered and which food gave away whole."

"I don't understand."

"I know you don't. Let's have some soup."

Agnes did not say much after the meal. Obviously she was tired of talking. I decided to go to bed.

While I was undressing, Agnes took the wolf doll and shook it several times by the scruff of the neck. She barked at it and jumped around it. I didn't have the slightest idea what she was doing, so I decided she was playing.

The following morning, in the first light, I followed Agnes outside. She pointed out various insects and told me which animals and birds ate them. Then she showed me plants, indicating which animals had a preference for each of them. She asked me to repeat it to her after she told me. Evidently I was going to get into a direct, pragmatic relationship with the knowledge she wanted to impart.

She wanted to know if I saw any game.

"No, nothing."

"Do you see grouse over there? That tree is full of squirrels. There are deer grazing beyond those rocks. Quail are over there, and soon ducks will fly overhead."

I hadn't seen any of the animals or birds she mentioned, but when I observed carefully, I saw that they were there.

"Yes, I see them," I said excitedly. "I would never have noticed any of them unless you showed me. Agnes, how can you see like that?"

"I know where to look. Develop hungry eyes—eyes that get hungry before your stomach. To be a huntress, you must have knowledge of what you are hunting. That's where hunting begins. You begin by learning how an animal acts. You have to see the game when others don't. A good hunter can always do this. I have seen this happen often—one hunter sees the game and the other doesn't. If you can't see the game, you have to know where it is in order to flush it. The important thing to remember is that you want to make a clean kill. How can you send an arrow without first seeing the game? It takes an even longer time to learn how to hunt a man. To hunt a man, a man who has power, you must use all your skill and do everything you can not to be deceived."

"Are you talking about Red Dog?" I asked.

"Yes, but you can't think about hunting such a powerful being at this time. Most beings just perform thoughtless actions—learn to hunt them first. Once you can hunt a thoughtless being with ease, then you can move on to more dangerous game. You must always learn of the hunted's powers. All creatures do this and that. Some cover their tracks and some don't. Some leave no trail, not the smallest blade of grass out of place. Some will leave blatant trails that will lead back into your own pitfalls. The more you can see, the more you can know about what other beings will do—the more chance you will have of being a successful huntress.

"There are good days to hunt and bad ones. There is usually some kind of game anywhere, some of it good, some of it not worth killing. Obviously, you have to go to the good places to get the game you want. As a huntress, you must never hesitate. You must analyze and then pounce, and to do that effectively you must know your own strength and weakness. Don't do anything stupid. Be the deliberate, stealthy huntress. The good huntress doesn't have a foolish opinion of herself. The good huntress kills. What does it mean to blow yourself up with pride and let your game get away? It's an insult to the hunted. The lost game has a right to go to the spirit house and ask for a spirit to be sent back to hunt you—either to kill you or drive you crazy. We know within us where the game lies, and our task is to kill it.

"Always be sure that you're the huntress and not the hunted. The path of the hunter is sacred. Never thoughtlessly kill anything—not even a bug. Imagine if something huge were to flatten *you* thoughtlessly. Kill only the game you can kill, and don't invade the territory of game that is smarter than you. Always approach your prey with reverence."

"Does that go for Red Dog?"

"Of course. He has what you want, and he knows all of these things. Approach any kill with reverence, grateful that you are the huntress and not the one to fall down."

I wanted to know more about hunting, but Agnes was finished. "I have to give you power to be effective," she said, "not ideas you don't know from your own inner voice, not borrowed knowledge. You want to have ability, don't you? You can't talk an animal to death."

Agnes started me looking, "seeing into the bush" as she called it.

For the next few days all I did was walk around. At the end of each day I was supposed to report to her the various animals I had seen. I was not supposed to think—to be pulled around by something other than my eyes. Agnes told me not to have a focal point, but to be ready for "tugs" that would lead me where I was supposed to go. By the fourth day, I could find pheasant in this manner.

Agnes was happy. "That's power," she said.

I was happy with my new ability as well.

I began to awaken to all sorts of animals. I saw deer, elk, antelope, skunks and rabbits. I sighted wild turkey and other game birds such as prairie chickens and grouse. I saw a beaver and two mink, and I was surprised once to confront a wolf. After we stared at each other for several minutes, I ran back to the cabin to tell Agnes.

"It says much," she said. "That was a medicine sign—a great blessing to you. Of all the animals in the bush, the wolf is the hardest to see, and it is virtually impossible to catch one. You must cut a lock of your hair and go back to the spot where you saw this wolf, and leave it there. That wolf didn't have to let you see him at all. He knew you were building power, and he came to help you!"

During this period, Agnes seemed reticent. Frequently she would cut me off when I said something and say, "Listen to yourself. I'm tired of it." I felt abandoned.

One night after dinner I said, "If I go hunting with my friends, they're going to get a surprise at all the game I'm able to spot."

"I don't want to hear about those murderers!" Agnes said.

"Murderers!" I blurted. "They're hunters just like you. Some people enjoy wild game."

"I said they were murderers. There is not one hunter among them. I've seen it many times. They come out here and shoot the hell out of the place. They have no respect for nesting birds—to them, hunting is murdering. They have no respect for life. They round up mustang and coyotes by helicopters and kill without honor. You should explain to those people that think they are better than the game they hunt that one day they, too, will die. The first place that kind of murderer goes in the faraway is to a clearing. The spirits of all the animals he has murdered circle him—whatever they are. They might be ducks or cats or bears.

"The spirits ask, 'Why did you kill us unfairly?' That idiot bastard better have a damn good answer, or those animals will rip him to shreds until they have their dignity back."

"Agnes, you're crazy," I said. "You made that up."

"You'll see whether I made it up or not when your giveaway comes. I'm telling you something I definitely know. I've told you many times that there is nothing without reason. There is justice—maybe not immediately, but the Great Spirit has forever to work it out. We humans just have this brief span until we fall down. I want to spend my days as a warrioress and recognize the beauty in all things. An animal is a child of the universe, like you and me. Taking the life of a wild and free animal should be done with the understanding of your own death. Otherwise, leave it be. The amazing thing is that these murderers don't even know enough to be embarrassed."

"Well, what is it I'm trying to learn how to do?" I asked in desperation.

"You are learning to hunt dangerous game, to do it bravely, fiercely, and with honor. You are walking even beyond that and learning how to steal power. If I saw that kind of murder in your heart, I would send you away and hope you went to your ancestors quickly."

I wish I could tell everything that I was taught in the following weeks. It would take many books to do it, and I will contemplate that time for the rest of my life.

One day she showed me crow tracks in a field.

"It is possible to track birds in the sky. The great trackers could do that. Even the sky leaves an image."

While she was talking, I somehow erased the crow track by standing on it. She gave me an icy look.

"I'm sorry," I said. "It was an accident."

"In the medicine world, there are no accidents," she said

furiously. "Every act has meaning. Can't you see that? That's what tracking is all about. *Accident* is a word born of confusion. It means we didn't understand ourselves enough to know why we did something. If you slip and cut your finger, there is a reason why you did it. Someone in your moon lodge wanted you to do it. If you knew how to listen to the chiefs inside your moon lodge, you would never do such a foolish thing. The medicine person never makes a mistake. A medicine woman knows how to send her scouts out from her moon lodge to look things over. When she gets to where she's going she knows what to expect, because her scouts have already been there and told her everything."

"I didn't plan to step on the tracks," I said.

"Yes, you did. I laugh when I hear the word *accident*. In all of the sacred grandparents' dreams, there was no confusion. Accident is a way to lay down the responsibility for your action and ask another to pick it up. If I slapped your face until you couldn't hear me, you wouldn't like it. Well, that's exactly what you've done, and I don't like it either."

I had never quarreled with Agnes, but that day I felt like it. The matter was complicated by the fact that whenever I doubted what Agnes had said and looked inside the deepest part of myself, invariably I found she was right.

The more I was taught, the less effective I seemed to become—I found myself moving hesitantly. My attempts to set snares, for instance, were very crude. Half the time, the snares I laid would trigger off by themselves. The other half, a tank wouldn't have set them off.

"I want you to set a snare at the watering place at Dead Man's Creek," Agnes said.

As we approached the watering place, Agnes pushed me back with her arm. "What are you doing wrong?" she asked.

I thought about it for a while. "I don't know."

"Which way is the wind blowing? You should approach the watering place so that your scent won't blow across the trail, downwind of the trail. We walked around the trail on the wrong side."

"Can animals really scent that well, Agnes?"

"People stink. These animals out here know the smell of humans real good."

Agnes and I waded upstream. I set the snare at the edge of the water, and Agnes had me rub strong-smelling leaves on the rawhide.

"That is the disguiser," she said. "Those leaves disguise your smell, you hope. What is the bait?"

"The water?"

"Yes, for this snare, the water is the bait. Would this snare catch anything?"

"I don't know."

"No, it wouldn't," Agnes said, pointing. "The loop is too wide and wouldn't catch. If it were built right, you might have a chance. You would never catch an old coyote down here in any snare. The old cunning ones know of the sacrifice. These animals will pretend to rush to the waterhole. The young animal, seeing the old one, rushes ahead in his greed and gets trapped.

"The most important thing about any trap is the bait. When you use water for bait, remember that it will be thirst that pulls the game. If you know the right bait, you can trap any being you want, but only if you know how to make the right trap as well. Learn the true character of an animal or a thing before you hunt it."

Learning how to hunt and all that it entailed—such as classifying and recognizing the different qualities of game animals—was a full-time occupation. Agnes had an inexhaustible knowledge of wildlife and hunting and arduous methods of communicating it. She had me tiptoe across the porch until I could show her that I could do it without making a sound. The task took me three days of painstaking effort to master, and by the end I knew every inch of the surface of the porch. I could finally step out from the edge and slip across in several different directions without a sound.

Agnes said that I was too contemplative. I was going to have to learn to be more aggressive. I spent all of my time out of doors, except at night. At times, Agnes seemed to be experimenting with me more than teaching me. Some days she would withhold food and water from me and make me work—chopping wood or carrying rocks—for no apparent reason. Talk was reduced to brief commands. I never argued—I became her total student. I tried to absorb as much knowledge as I could.

One evening during this period, I burst through the cabin door and ran headlong into Hyemeyohsts Storm. I was startled to see him there.

The table was covered with a chief's blanket, and on top of it was a large shield, the most beautiful I had ever seen. A train of perfectly matched hawk feathers trailed down, nearly touching the floor. Agnes was sitting cross-legged close to the table, examining the feathers attached to the train.

"What in the world are you doing here, Hyemeyohsts?"

"I was showing Agnes a medicine shield. I wanted her advice on something. Agnes is like a grandmother to me, and don't I have a right to visit my own family?"

I said something inarticulate in reply.

"How do you like the shield?" Hyemeyohsts wanted to know.

"I didn't know shields were made this way. I've never seen anything so breathtaking."

"There were once many shields like this," Agnes said, "but they were hidden or destroyed. Very few people have the privilege of seeing a true medicine shield."

There was a great blue eagle painted in the center. The leather was stretched tight, possibly antelope hide, and there were eagle feathers on the rim. The hawk feather train was about four feet long, with feathers on either side. You could feel power coming from it.

Hyemeyohsts carefully moved the shield to the bed and we had some coffee. We talked for a while, Hyemeyohsts showing Agnes several beaded medicine wheels of various colors and patterns. Agnes moved them around on the chief's blanket in different arrangements, the movements apparently having some hidden meaning.

Hyemeyohsts pointed. "If you look into the circles you will begin to perceive the great medicine circle. The smaller circles are your teachings. These medicine wheels are also like shields."

Agnes lifted one of the beaded wheels and held it to her heart, then returned it to the table with the others.

"Those medicine wheels are rings of meaning if you find your eyes," Hyemeyohsts went on. "Taken together, they are pieces of a puzzle. Like the great medicine snake eating its own tail, they will dream you through the dream. They are segments in the mandala of your life and mine. If you ever once fit the circles together so that they reflect the great medicine circle, you will be free of illusion. You will have performed your act of power, your true purpose in life. Within that act is your death, and in your death you will find your true circle. But you are not ready for these teachings."

Agnes had me do some work around the cabin, and afterward I was so tired I curled up on the bed next to the beautiful shield and fell asleep until morning. When I awoke, Hyemeyohsts had covered me with his blanket, but the shield was gone and so was he.

So many days passed that I lost count. I suspected that Agnes was dissatisfied with my progress. Late one afternoon, after a full day of tracking a deer, we were sitting watching the sunset, both quiet in the grandeur of the evening.

"Tomorrow morning," Agnes suddenly said, "you will see if you have the stealth to steal the basket. You can go to Red Dog's and give it a try."

I was taken aback, particularly since I didn't feel that I had learned more that a tiny amount of what Agnes had been attempting to teach me. I thought that perhaps I was going to have to spend years as her initiate. I felt I needed more time. I tried to say something, but nothing came out.

"No, you are not ready," Agnes said, "but I don't know what else I can do. I can't spend forever teaching you things. The dreamers think you have power, and it's time to see if they are right."

"Agnes," I said in agony. "I'm more confused now than when I first started. How will I be able to do it without knowing more? I still don't know the first thing about what you're teaching me."

"You know more than you think you do. I am teaching you to be a being of stealth."

"But what is that?"

"A being of stealth is a credible being. You wouldn't know a stealthy being if you saw one. But then—that's the way we like it."

"Well, Agnes, you may think this is a stupid question, but are you a stealthy being?"

"It is not a stupid question, since you cannot see that I am. A being of stealth can enter a room and do what she wants. She can leave the room when she wants to. Most beings who enter a room are led and confused, but a being of stealth can enter and leave any room that she wants to. A being of stealth counted coup on you and took what he wanted. A being of stealth is dangerous and not afraid to strike. This being will move differently than you think unless you too are a stealthy being. A stealthy being knows of its death."

"Well, am I getting close to becoming a stealthy being?"

I had never seen Agnes laugh so hard. Her face dripped with tears, and she slapped me on the back.

"I've done what I can," she said finally. "That's why you're here. If you can steal the basket, that would be a stealthy act, the act of a great warrioress. The better the huntress, the more dangerous the game. A man like Red Dog is more dangerous than almost any spirit. To hunt down a man like Red Dog and then to rob his lair—I would say that if you can do it, you are very close to becoming a stealthy being."

"But not now?"

"No. Not yet. This bush country is still new to you. Stealth means power, and you are still a blunderer. A blunderer who sets traps rarely makes a good catch. Blunderers catch other blunderers. Stupid beings live on each other, but don't let that fool you.

Stealthy beings can be any place at any time, and you can wait for a stealthy being forever and never see one. Only a stealthy being can see another stealthy being. A stealthy being has dreams that are real.

"No barrier will stop a stealthy being. Where the footsteps of the stealthy being disappear, you see a crow or a balloon or an eagle, but what you are really seeing is a stealthy being levitating. The problem with the incapable beings is that they never look at the multiple parts of the tangled trails. They have no knowledge, and that is good—they wouldn't know what to do with it if they had it.

"Once in a while, incapable beings find important pieces. Watch out when they do. They say 'Ah ha! It's so simple.' That's when you're on the trail to power and you pick up the first glittering thing you see. When you are on the trail to being stealthy and see glittering things, you should lift up your eyes and pass by all of them.

"When an incapable being makes a scintillating discovery and picks up the glittering thing, it's all over for him. He is cursed. The dust kicks up around him in mighty swells, and he hears voices from the far-away. He is not a complete hunter. He appears humble, but he becomes obsessed with his own importance. Other beings see the incapable being who has made the scintillating discovery and are fascinated. Most likely, the incapable being causes havoc and ruin. He goes about, pushing his way anywhere he wants to go, but he has no stealth. He has the power of a young bull, and he might become a king or ruler, or a religious leader, but he is never the complete hunter. He can only lead you as far as he has gone, and why shouldn't he? He thinks the scintillating discovery is all there is. He holds it to his chest and roars out over the land, and the people all come and look, smearing themselves with his false paint. They put on his beadwork and follow him to their destruction.

"You probably think you wouldn't follow an incapable being, but don't laugh. I could send you away with a scintillating discovery right now. You could have all the great baskets that have ever been, except one. Or I could trick you and say I'm giving you the marriage basket, and you would go away happy, but you wouldn't have it—you would have the disguiser. But I won't give up on teaching you. I wouldn't trick you about that. I want you to have what you came for. I want you to have the marriage basket more than anything. In fact, it probably means more to me than you know."

First you must realize you are in danger.

—Author

It had begun.

As I watched, a haze of pearl gray light settled around Red Dog's cabin. I lay flat on my stomach under a mulberry bush covered with leaves, my face blackened with pigments ground from the river clay. The odors of the earth were strong in my nostrils. I waited tensely. Ants crawled over and around me, probing my skin for food. It was unbearable, but I didn't dare move. I had been there two days.

The magical palace of Red Dog, I thought to myself. How could anyone with power enough to kill me and harbor the marriage basket live like that? The cabin was rectangular and squat, and looked unattended. Clumps of mud and old newspapers chinked spaces between logs. The tin roof was rusty and full of holes patched with green and red tar paper. The small windows were so greasy I couldn't see inside. A rooster and chickens clucked behind the cabin around the toolshed, which appeared to be partially buried in the solid, sloping ground.

Ben and Drum kept coming outside to the toolshed, where they would heave open the heavy door and be lost for several minutes. I could hear them clanking around, pounding and scraping. Ben would stand leaning in the doorway, making sarcastic remarks.

"Drum, you're sure you know how to use a nail, aren't you?" he would say, dropping a burning cigarette to the ground and stamping on it. "It's not too much for you, is it?"

Drum would come back out with tools or lengths of rope and go about the grounds finding things, while Ben followed behind in a supervisory manner. They cleaned out pieces of rusting machinery, dug holes and put something like garbage in them, sometimes punched each other playfully and made hooting jokes. Sometimes they would just stand together. Both seemed to do as little work as possible.

The outhouse was a tilting affair with a rusty spring-loaded door that squeaked open and shut in the wind with an annoying persistence. I thought of Red Dog's cabin as The Dump because every manner of rusting, rickety, rotting accoutrement was left at random, wedged into the ground as if planted there some forty years ago. An old plow that should have been bronzed lay on its back yawning at the sky. There were several overgrown piles of old tires for the rooster to climb on and crow to his heart's content. He was lord of The Dump and let everyone know it.

Off to the right behind a falling-down fence were two thin cows, their hip bones nearly poking through their skin. Patches of their hair were missing, their udders appeared to be dry of milk, and the bells that hung around their necks clanged as they ate their meager food.

An old Model T Ford lay on its side stripped of everything, including its axle. A tattered hammock strung between the back bumper of the car and the side of the privy flapped in the wind.

When Ben and Drum banged the front door of the cabin open, it made me jump. They went out to use the privy or pee off the front porch, but Red Dog seemingly had no need to relieve himself. I never once saw him, and I wasn't even sure he was there. For two days, the only noises I had heard were the cow bells, chickens, and slamming of the cabin and privy doors.

Late in the afternoon of the second day, suddenly, an insane yowling came from within the cabin. My hair stood on end— leaves and all. First there was a high screeching sound like a screech owl, again and again, then something like the lament of a prehistoric creature. Then moments later, a shrill moan was repeated many times and a low, growling sound answered. These sounds went on for a long time, but I never saw their source.

Just as suddenly it was quiet again. All I heard were the trembling leaves and the high wind sweeping over the tableland. I was about to shut my eyes and doze when I heard a crashing sound, then a quick stomping of feet. I saw a gray mouse run out from beneath the cabin door, scurry across the porch, and run over to a jutting rock. Then the door was thrown open and first Drum, then Ben ran outside and looked around.

"Where the hell is he?" Drum asked.

"There he is."

Ben and Drum pursued the mouse all around the yard, trying to corner it. The mouse scurried up a tree, leapt to the tin roof and down a post. The mouse was fast and tricky, and Ben and Drum couldn't get near enough to catch him. Whenever it looked as if he was done for, he would choose the least expected maneuver, surface some place else, and squeak in delight.

"Over yonder," Ben yelled.

Ben and Drum ran to a point where the mouse had reemerged into the yard, waited until they were almost upon him, and then set off running again. The tiny creature tripped up Ben and Drum at every turn.

Then it appeared the mouse had made a fatal mistake—he ran inside a rusted tin can. Drum dove for the can and put his hand over the mouth.

"I got him! I got him!"

"Let me see. Let me see, Drum."

Drum spread his fingers enough to look inside and he shook the can. He looked again.

"Is he in there?"

"He's got to be in there," Drum said. "I saw him."

He looked again and shook the can. "Hell, he ought to be in there, but I don't see him."

"He got away," Ben said. "There's no way we're going to catch him."

Drum shook the can again, harder and harder, and turned it over as if to empty it. "Not in here," he said.

Just then, the mouse dropped from the can onto the ground. Drum and Ben shouted, and the chase began once more. The mouse ran along the side of the cabin and toward the privy, turned around, and ran between Ben's legs. Ben leapt away in mock horror. Then the mouse ran to the edge of the trees and waited.

"Screw you," Drum called.

"Yeah, screw you," Ben agreed.

The mouse swiveled its head, looking at them with black button eyes. Very calmly, it went to the toolshed and under the door.

"There's no way out of there, Drum," Ben said. "He's trapped now."

Both of them ran as fast as they could to the shed and went inside.

"Plug up the door," I heard Ben say.

Then there was a noise like nothing I had ever heard before—like the roar of a fiend. Ben and Drum burst out of the shed and ran down the road as if they had seen the devil himself. The mouse came out and went back in the cabin, but it was almost a half hour before Ben and Drum returned.

Later, though there was no sound from behind the cabin door, I saw a pale orange light burning through the window. Fingers of the last evening sun walked across the tiers of logs. There was still no sign of Red Dog, but I wasn't going to make my move until I knew for sure that he was gone.

The light inside the cabin went out, the cabin door opened, and Ben and Drum stood whispering to each other in the deep shadows of the porch. Then they walked off down the road, singing. I watched their silhouettes disappear over the hill, and their singing faded away. I was cold and tense. I reasoned that the candle would still be burning if someone was inside—this was the moment I had been waiting for. Now I could go to the cabin and steal the basket. All the while I had been observing the cabin, Red Dog hadn't even been there! How foolish I had been.

There wasn't a sound, except for the squeaking privy door. Even the chickens were quiet. I rubbed my thighs and curled my toes to get the circulation moving. I was stiff. As the wind blew across my face I crept forward slowly without making a sound. I started to shiver. Somehow I crossed the hundred yards to the cabin, and crouched flat against the log wall. There was the sooty smell of coal oil. It was getting darker by the moment, and misshapen shadows were protruding in irregular lengths. I listened for a few minutes, then went forward and waited again—listening and looking. Anxiety swept over me. I had the feeling that I was about to be murdered.

My back to the wall, I inched my hands over the rough exterior of the logs and forced my way forward to the window. Inching up, I placed my hands on the sill—feeling it, trying to perceive the contents of the cabin. Nothing. I turned and peered over the edge. The panes were covered with grime and reflected the sky. I wiped a circle with the sleeve of my sweatshirt, cupped my hands over my eyes, and placed them on the cool pane. There was total darkness. I tried to focus my eyes but couldn't see anything. If Red Dog was in there, he knew I was about to break in. I gathered all my will and walked to the door, the single thought of the marriage basket on my mind. I slowly turned the knob and opened the door a crack.

I was quivering in terror.

From the road, I heard the crazed barking of a dog—it sounded savage. I shut the door as quietly as I had opened it, then panicked. I turned and raced noiselessly back across the yard to my thicket of trees and bushes, dove, and submerged myself beneath leaves and earth.

The dog was on the porch, snarling and snapping. Then I heard soft canine footsteps. I could see his eyes as he sniffed right toward me, growling. I quit squirming and became very still.

Drum's voice boomed out. "Shut up, Soup Bone!"

"He probably has a skunk treed over there," Ben said.

"I don't care, I don't like that damned noise. It'll wake up Red Dog and then watch out. It'll be our ass."

"Come on, Soup Bone," Ben called to the dog.

They both whistled, and the dog, who had been ready to bite me, reluctantly turned around and trotted back toward the cabin with an occasional bark.

"YOU IDIOTS! TIE THAT MONGREL UP BEFORE I KILL YOU! I'M TRYING TO SLEEP!"

It was Red Dog's voice from within the cabin. He had actually been in there.

The night was silent from then on, and nothing stirred around the cabin the next day. Not even the rooster crowed.

Toward evening the drumming began. The beat was irritating—not at all the way Agnes and Ruby played. The sound seemed to skim over the land and collect in pockets. It seemed to have no reason, except to stun the air. The drumming went on for a while, and I thought I heard the braying of a jackass. Then the ground around the cabin shook, I heard the sound of hooves on boards, and there was a tumultuous racket. Next the braying and drumming stopped, the cabin door slowly opened, and standing in the doorway was Red Dog.

He looked like a disheveled mountain man. He was wearing old khaki trousers and an olive-drab field jacket, his red hair was shoulder length, and he had a long beard. His eyes had the same piercing glint as those of an eagle. I was shaking. Was it my imagination, or could I feel his strength from that distance?

He held a silver object that glimmered like a knife in the setting sun. He closed the cabin door, walked to the edge of the porch, and sat down. Despite his heavy boots, he made no noise. My gaze fixed on those big boots, then moved to the knife that he was lifting to his mouth, as though to lick something off the blade. I realized that the knife was actually a flute. He held it poised to his lips for a moment, then a sweet, delicate music came forth. I began to relax. Red Dog threw back his head, his eyes closed, and played with abandon. The ordinary world was disappearing around me as I listened.

I closed my eyes, then opened them quickly to see more clearly. Again, I noticed the conspicuous boots. They were a strange, wheat-brown color, their texture almost feathery. They seemed to be splitting open. I realized that below the knee his legs were becoming covered with feathers.

Red Dog rose, his legs wide apart. The fluting was louder now, even more melodic. With a great burst of energy he leapt into the air. It was as if he was breaking free of the earth. He cocked his head, then bent at the waist, whirled, and somehow became the image of the fierce katchina spirit Kokopelli. There was a white painted stripe down the center of his giant mask-like head. The rest of his face, except for white circles above the eyes, was black. Feathers, both red and white, crowned his forehead, and a phallic nose thrust out beaklike toward me. A necklace like a fat black and white snake coiled around his neck. I caught a glimpse of a sack slung over his shoulder.

For a moment I could not look at him. He was humpbacked and grotesque in the failing light, both ugly and beautiful. His blue rattle gleamed, his flute trilled. He cavorted around the cabin, swirling and dancing. He bounded to the roof, then leapt perilously close and circled me. I realized he had known I was there all along. He smiled at me, an arrogant smile of love. From the sack on his back he took out a ring and offered it to me, teasing me, leaping in a fury from side to side with his painted arm outstretched. I was being enchanted. He leaned forward, and I could feel his hot breath on me. I adored him. He embodied the spirits of all the katchinas. He beckoned. He taunted me, turning his sensual body slowly so that I wanted to reach out and touch him. The music coaxed me, and I could hear myself uttering faint sighing noises. I became aware of an oppressive heat. We were ringed with light and shadows.

"I'll go with you," I whispered, starting to rise. I took a step. Then a powerful hand gripped my arm and I swung around in terror. I was looking squarely into the furious eyes of Agnes.

"Come with me," she demanded, hissing the words in my ear.

"No!" I screamed.

I was insane with passion. I struggled for a moment, trying to kick Agnes and wrench free of her grasp. I looked around wildly for the Kokopelli, but only caught a glimpse of Red Dog sitting on the porch in his khaki clothes, exactly the way he had been. I was hysterical. I kicked and clawed at Agnes' face. She swung at me and connected.

I awoke lying on her bed in the cabin. My own whining and moaning had awakened me. My head was swollen and ached where Agnes had hit me and knocked me out. She stood over me, a look of utter disdain on her wrinkled face, her eyes flashing. She stamped her foot.

"You didn't wear it," she yelled. She held up her hand and dangled my antler earring. "She couldn't find you. You were nearly lulled to your death. If you had followed that mirage, Red Dog would have slipped off with your spirit."

"I meant to wear it," I stammered. "I forgot."

"I hope you don't die. Now, young lady, you will have to face the passions of Red Dog."

Sorcerers never kill anybody. They make people kill themselves.
                                        —Agnes Whistling Elk

I couldn't eat. I was pacing around the cabin. The walls, the roof—everything weighed on me. Agnes sat in her usual chair, watching every move I made.

"Agnes, stop staring at me," I said.

Agnes said nothing as I walked back and forth, back and forth. I could hear the strains of the Kokopelli's flute in my right ear. My passion was driving me mad.

"Why can't I just go talk with Red Dog, Agnes?" I asked. "Maybe we could come to some understanding." My voice had the whine of a spoiled schoolgirl.

"No," Agnes said flatly. Then she added, "Try to understand. Red Dog is changing the bait. He's making himself the bait. Red Dog has been naughty, and he should have his ass kicked."

I hadn't even heard Agnes' words. I stamped my foot and glared at her. I had to get some breathing space.

"Can I go sit on the porch?"

"No."

"Why not?"

"No. Absolutely not."

"Please, Agnes."

"No. That's final."

"Oh, all right."

The notes of the pipe made me think of the lustful smile of Kokopelli. I smiled contritely and apologized for my adolescent behavior. Agnes nodded.

A half hour of torture passed. When I could contain myself no longer, I said, "I'm going to go to the car and get a book I left in the trunk."

Agnes didn't reply.

"It's an interesting book of yoga, Agnes," I said, opening the door. "It's by a friend of mine. You'll enjoy the pictures."

I took a few steps outside the cabin and then ran up the path toward the car. Halfway there, I stopped and looked back. Agnes was nowhere to be seen. I heaved a sigh. "I got away from you, you old bat!"

I walked off smugly and turned left onto a path to Red Dog's place. I was losing my grip on everything, but I didn't care. The flute music grew louder, luring me, and I started to run. I turned a corner in the path between two large rocks and stopped abruptly.

"Agnes," I gasped in fright. "I was just . . . "

She was blocking my way. Her hand shot out and jerked me sideways and around.

"Get back to that cabin," she said. She was furious.

I stumbled back to the cabin waiting for another chance to bolt.

"Sit on the bed and be quiet," she ordered, when we were inside. "You're so stupid, the next time I'll let him finish you."

My insides were burning. It was as though Red Dog had put an itch in me. It was all I could do not to run again.

Agnes was rummaging around in the trunk looking for something, her back turned. I broke for the door, but Agnes grabbed my flying hair and yanked me sprawling back onto the bed. I started to howl and sob.

"Lynn, compel yourself to think," I heard Agnes say.

But the flute music was like a cathedral organ resounding in my brain. I was foaming at the mouth. I kicked and scratched and tried to bite Agnes.

"I hate you!" I screamed. "I hate you! Let me go or you'll be sorry!"

Agnes had what she was looking for inside the trunk. She held a length of rope in her hand and another in her teeth. She caught my two wrists as if she were bulldogging a calf and secured them to the head of the bed. Then she looped the rope and tied my feet to the foot of the bed, stood up, and dusted her hands together.

"There," she said.

I clenched and unclenched my fingers, struggled and raved. Then the clouds in my head began to clear a little.

"Agnes, really," I said finally, trying to sound dignified. "I'm a logical person. Can't we discuss this situation without all this melodrama? These ropes are hurting me."

"Yes, and the more you fight them the tighter they'll get."

She pulled her chair over next to the bed and sat down. With closed eyes, she sang a sweet song in Cree, but I was too angry to care.

"Do you know this is against the law? I can have you put in jail for this."

She laughed.

"I don't care about the damned basket anymore. Everything is pulling me apart. I just want to know that man." I started to cry. "I can't stand it."

"Listen to me!" Agnes yelled with such a singular command that the visions and even the music stopped for that instant. "Listen to me," she repeated again. Somehow her voice penetrated my confusion. "You don't know what you're up against. Think about July. I want to tell you about her. July is Ruby's apprentice, just as you are mine. One day, she was walking down the road, hitchhiking into Crowley. She saw an old pickup truck coming down the road and turned to stick out her thumb as it pulled up next to her. She was surprised to see a brand new car. She thought her memory was playing tricks on her. The white man who was driving was very courteous and offered her a lift. July got in. The man said he was a rancher on the reserve, and that he was scouting for Indian hands to help round up cattle. July said that she would try to think of someone who could do that kind of work. When July was sitting there, there was something strange about the man. She happened to look down at the floor of the car and saw that the foot on the accelerator was a cloven hoof. She looked back up at him and he started to blur in her vision. Her eyes couldn't focus, but she knew it wasn't the same man. She knew that she had walked into a sorcerer's trap, that it was Red Dog. She tried to put up her shields, but it was too late for that. All she could do was scream for him to let her out. She didn't expect Red Dog to let her go, but he pulled over and stopped. When she threw open the door and started running, she heard him call her name, 'July.' Then she heard the music of the flute. She didn't want to, but she had to stop and turn around. He had her in his power, and she walked back to him in a trance. July had no more will."

Agnes quit talking and there was a long silence. I swallowed hard and asked, "What happened then?"

"Have you ever seen a spider kill a butterfly?"

"No, I haven't," I said.

"Well, that's very much what happened to July. The spider played games with her. He didn't kill her off quick with a merciful sting. He danced around her with his flute, torturing her with his music, just like he's doing to you. And like the spider with the butterfly, he slowly sucked her insides out. She became his lover. He carried off her spirit and her power along with it, put it in a gourd, and hung it up in his cabin. It's a big joke to that bastard. When he was through with her, he took her and dumped her on Ruby's porch. All he left her with was that old flute. She is still possessed by the music, and that's why she repeats it all the time. Ruby was furious. The hills around her cabin shook for days, and the animals in the forest were afraid to come out. Red Dog has been laughing ever since." Her voice became vindictive. "Ruby's going to get him, you wait and see. She's going to de-bone one of his apprentices. So, Lynn, this is what you're faced with."

Agnes' face was serious. She felt my forehead, and it dawned on me that I was ill, that I had been separated from my sanity. The knowledge of what had happened to July settled in on me. I started to shake with fear, thinking of her vacant, mad stare.

I heard the fluting music again. Wave after wave of passion swept over me. It was as if Red Dog realized he was losing his grip on me and was coming in for the kill. Agnes took down a tied rawhide pouch from the wall, opened it, took what looked like crushed leaves, and rolled them into a cigarette. Lighting it, she took several puffs and came over. She sat on my chest.

"Smoke this sacred smoke," she demanded, holding my chin and guiding the cigarette to my lips. "Lynn, this will help you dream. Dream your passion. Fly away. Go through the hoop of your innermost fears and desires. Meet them and conquer them. Come through your own reflection and be free of Red Dog. Act in your dreams as you want to act and find the guarded kivas where you have hidden your heart."

The last thing I remember was Agnes unstraddling me and sitting back down at the table. My eyes were shut. The tantalizing strains of the flute lazed through my mind. The low roof started to spin, then faded like a veil. I shot out of my body and outside the cabin. For a moment, I walked around through the trees, then squatted down to look at a pebble on the ground. It appeared to have a hole in it. After staring at it intently, I made myself very small in order to follow a minuscule light shining from within the hole.

As I entered the hole, I heard a violent cracking sound and then, suddenly, I was flying very fast through cold, crystalline space. After a time, I came to a vast moonlit courtyard surrounded by a jungle. In the center was the Grand Jaguar Temple. Two pyramids erected from giant hand-hewn rocks were set facing each other several hundred yards apart. Between them, there was a raised altar of stone. This was the place of the jaguar, the place of the balance of forgetting and remembering.

The silence awakened with the piping of the flute and the soft sound of moccasins over grass. Silhouetted against the south pyramid, the fantastic figure of the Kokopelli danced and whirled. His dance was an ancient ceremony, his pipe played the mating call of the dream. Red Dog was reaching me on some inner plane, and an answering passion was awakened in me.

The giant pyramids grew clearer and clearer as the moon rose. The cabin and Agnes had completely disappeared from my mind, and the brilliant night sky of another time was overhead. The great katchina remained a silvery irresistible figure in the moonlight. He danced and played his magnificent flute, twisting and beckoning toward the altar. I stood at the top of the pyramid with my white robes flowing in the hot wind. We had slipped through a crevice between the worlds—a dimension that concerned the highest things of the mind, a dimension of magic. I was possessed by love for the Kokopelli, and we were performing a sacred ceremony that would bring power to the everlasting flow of life. I was the symbol of all women.

I walked slowly down the pyramid steps. The katchina man was sitting on the altar looking part animal, part bird, part human, winking at me. I was walking toward my death, but I didn't care. The Kokopelli brought me closer with his gleaming eyes, reached out his arms to hold me, and settled me gently back on the altar.

It was covered with sweet-smelling sage, and two torches flamed at either end. The play of torchlight and darkness was hypnotic. I could scarcely breathe. His face glowed—changing, disappearing, reappearing. I closed my eyes and became aware of what was neither him nor me, but the power of the dream that stood behind us both. It was a union of the higher and lower selves and we were made one with all cosmic life. The flute seemed to play on by itself. As we lay on the stone altar, the hot night breeze blowing over us like an astral blanket, I looked up into the face of the Kokopelli and realized that I lay there alone—that by possessing him whom I had feared and wanted most, we had merged into one being, warrior and warrioress. I had mated with the warrior—the male—in myself.

The pyramids disappeared, and I felt myself whisked away. I curled into the fetal position—naked and whirling out of time. Everything went dark.

I awoke shivering and shaking. Agnes had untied the ropes. She brought a bucket and I threw up. Then she pulled her chair over and sat with me as I lay back, feeling very weak. I looked out the window and saw that the rays of the sun were low in the west. It was late into the next day.

Agnes brushed back my hair and felt my forehead. "How do you feel?" she asked. Something between mirth and gravity showed on her face. "Are we going to have a baby kachina?"

She giggled.

I related what happened as best I could. I realized as I spoke that I now felt only a residue of passion. My sanity seemed restored.

"Agnes," I said, feeling able to sit up at last. "What does all this, the dream, have to do with the marriage basket?"

"They touch each other in your state of remembering. You became aware that the marriage basket was conceived by the dreamers to signify the union between the high warrior and high warrioress within your own being. Every woman seeks after that high warrior, that most magnificent of men, within her. We seek him all our lives. If we're lucky, we conjure him in our dreams, mate with him, and become whole. Do you understand me?"

"Yes, I think so, yes."

"Those two-chief dreams are great luck. You had to trick power to find it. Its symbol is big medicine, medicine that woman has forgotten. It was greatly dangerous, but now you can help them remember that medicine. You have smoked the male and female within your lodge-self and you have come to a place where the roads fork. You can change and grow. You begin to understand what it really means to yield. Woman thinks she yields, but she has forgotten how. Many women's lodges stand deserted because no one looks inside.

"Reach out for that high warrior waiting in the woman's lodge. Embrace him and be free."

The orange sun looked like an oblong egg lowering into twilight. We sat outside silently. I was still trembling, and I had a queasy feeling in the pit of my stomach. Later, when it was dark, Agnes told me to go back to bed. She said it would be a while until I was fully recovered from my experiences. She didn't come in until later, and I woke to see her in the chair by the bedside. Her hands were clasped in her lap. She was looking straight ahead at the patterns of light on the wall.

"Good night," I said.

She smiled at me and motioned me back to sleep.

What are your night visions or your pain but the failure of your will?
—Hyemeyohsts Storm

When I sat up in bed, I felt as if I had been on a week-long binge. The sacred smoke was very powerful, I walked very slowly to the table and sat down.

Agnes was sorting out a bewildering variety of things: rocks, crystals, a rope of sweet grass, a turtle shell, some kind of bleached jawbone, feathers, pressed flowers, and other things I couldn't recognize.

"Everything is alive, Lynn. I have watched the spirit of whiskey take many. The spirit of plants or drugs have taken many. There are very few who know the spirit of anything, but that's the thing to learn. It can be a perilous meeting, but I hope that we can journey together and that I can lead you there when you know enough. Eat," she said.

We fixed some breakfast, but I could hardly eat a bite. I sipped some tea and the warmth made me feel a little better.

"Agnes, that experience last night or whenever it was—yesterday—seemed as real as any I've ever had. I believe that I met Red Dog as a Kokopelli katchina somewhere."

She held a leaf up to the morning light and examined it. "Don't you think the moon lodge is real?" she asked suddenly. She started stacking the rocks and crystals inside the curve of the bleached jawbone. "Dreams are diving down deep in the earth. They are feminine in character. Male takes the substance and forms it. Dreams are your other-half vision. Don't you think you are real? This time you brought back power. This time you remembered."

"I am very confused about dreams," I said. "And what they are and what they mean. My dreams in the last few months have seemed very real and seem to have affected my life totally. I can't conceive of dreams having substance, though. Even this one. This one seems more like a vision."

"Has it ever occurred to you that the human is teetering between two worlds of reflection? Touch the earth, for the mother is awake. The earth is alive and dreaming. Everything the human can think of has substance. There are no holes in your thoughts. The awake ones, the shamaness can wander to the other side of the universe, beyond even the far-away. Here appears the rainbow door to the backward web of substance. If you invade that world, the beings there can give you any power you want. Most powers are too heavy to bring back. How glad we are if we can get back through that door once it's been opened to us. But the greatest warriors have counted coup there many times. You came here through that door the moment you were conceived and you are sucked back through it the moment you die. That is where it is all given and that is where it is all taken away. The keepers want you to come there and take what you can. When you enter, they recognize you and sing and chant. You speak of substance. Listen, every substance, including my dreams, is my sister and my brother, and I recognize them and we live here gently."

"Agnes," I said. "I just got up."

Agnes laughed. "The problem with you is that many teachings have been revealed to you in your lifetime, and you haven't been awake enough to see them."

"At least I've learned some things," I said indignantly.

"Lynn, you've tripped over an eagle feather as if it were blocking your path."

"What does that mean?"

"You think I'm a crazy old lady, and I am." She laughed loudly.

I protested. "I wouldn't be here if I thought that, would I?"

"You might." She laughed again.

"You still haven't told me what you mean by tripping over an eagle feather."

"An eagle soars above and sees all the vast complexities and interrelationships. When an eagle feather falls from a medicine eagle to the earth, it is full of that knowledge. If you're smart, you will talk to that eagle feather and ask the spirit of it to guide you. All eagle feathers have that power. You have to pick it up and talk to it. Then you have to know how to listen to the answer. Eat your breakfast."

I forced myself to eat while Agnes put away her collection of goods in the dresser. She shut the drawer and stared at me thoughtfully.

"Come on, Lynn," she said.

I followed her out onto the front porch. July was slouched back against the post, playing the flute. I realized that I had heard the flute so often, so continually, that I had blotted it out of my mind. Now that I listened, the sound was weak and flagging. There wasn't much breath behind it.

"Sit down right here," Agnes said, indicating a spot on the porch floor directly in front of July. I sat down with infinite care, my body a lot stiffer than I realized. Agnes squatted between us and took July's chin in her hand.

"Look carefully at July, Lynn," she said. "Look into her eyes and tell me what you see. Describe her."

I had been so busy I hadn't noticed how diminished she had become. She was unaware of our presence, and she kept dropping the flute from her mouth and drooling. She was terribly pale and emaciated, her brown eyes more sunken and vacant than ever.

"I see someone who has lost her mind," I stammered.

Agnes probed me with her eyes. "Do you want that to happen to you?"

"No," I cried. "I don't."

"Then stay here and watch her for a while," Agnes said. "You may still end up like that." She went back inside.

Left alone, I leaned my back against the wall, trying to clear my head. July was fumbling around for her flute. I thought over the encounter she had had with Red Dog, and it brought tears of pity to my eyes. But at the thought of Red Dog, a pang of jealousy stabbed through me—I felt like a she-wolf with her territory invaded and, for an instant, I hated July. I couldn't seem to control my thoughts. Maybe I was the one who was crazy. I wondered if July was thinking that she was the only one who was free, because she heard Red Dog's music.

"Lynn, have you seen enough?" It was Agnes.

"Yes, I think so. Agnes, does she hear Red Dog's flute music? Why does she try to blow those notes all the time?"

"There's no noise in July's head, no images or anything. She is a sick person and may die. Red Dog will never return her spirit. She blows her flute because she has to. Why does the moon go about the earth the way it does? July is caught in a maze. If you touch her with other things, you are flirting with catastrophe."

I shuddered. "Isn't there anything we can do to help her?"

"There is nothing you can do. Maybe I can do something, but then . . . " Agnes left the sentence unfinished. "Come back into the cabin," she said.

Agnes took my arm and pulled me inside. The light seemed dim.

"I see that July disgusts you," Agnes said.

"No, I feel sorry for her—that's all."

Agnes' face remained impassive. "Listen, July will be dead inside a week. Pretty soon, her spirit will forget her discarded body and annihilate her. You take care you don't join her. Red Dog still intends to teach you his viewpoint. That's his viewpoint sitting out on my porch."

"I can't seem to control my desires, Agnes."

"Lynn, there are shaman spirit-suckers. They do it by sex and our instinct for it. They siphon off your spirit as if it were nothing. Sing away from them like an arrow sings. Cut a path to the outer rims and leap to your end, rather than getting caught by that kind of shaman man. Red Dog is trying to bend you to his course."

"Does Red Dog really have July's spirit somewhere?" I blurted. "What does that mean?"

"I told you so," Agnes said.

She leaned forward and her eyes flashed out at me like a lizard's.

"I can crack you right in two," she said. "Humans are not twins of themselves—you know, right and left. Both your sides are different and serve different purposes. There is a seam down the middle. A medicine man or woman can see the seam and break you right into two parts. It's easy. Red Dog uses sex to do it. You see, Lynn, I could have sex with Red Dog, and for me that act would be a gathering of power."

"Like in my dream of the katchina man?"

"Yes, like the nature of your dream. Red Dog would even be a good man for me if I could stand him. But as far as I'm concerned, that crazy bastard is too ugly to look at. With you, you are not strong enough for him yet. The power of the warrior and warrioress would not manifest. You would break in half and be nothing."

"I would die?"

"When you are cracked in two, that's when a shaman can take you—take your spirit."

"Does a spirit look like anything?"

"Like smoke."

"There's actually something inside a person that looks like smoke, and this is the spirit?"

"Yes, like a puff of tobacco smoke. We would all be dead if it weren't for tobacco smoke. With tobacco smoke, the two-leggeds slipped by death. Death saw the wind taking up smoke, thought it was the spirits he wanted, and went away."

"Is that what Red Dog has in his gourd—that part of July that looks like smoke?"

"Exactly. That's what she has to get back if she wants to live."

"Can you make him give her spirit back?"

"You can't make Red Dog do anything. No one can budge him if he doesn't want to move."

"What happens when a person dies, Agnes?"

"It's not an important question. The whole of a human's life is watched by the thunder chiefs. You have a road within you, a turquoise road. The important thing is to keep your spirit moving along this road. If you do that, in the end of your days you will merge with the thunder chiefs. All your other roads lead back into absurdity and delusion. Those roads swell with pain, sorrow, and confusion. I have a little power because I see through to the end. In the end, all the riddles solve and the paradoxes are answered. In the end, the meaning of your tears and suffering is clear. And if you find it in your time, you will be full and no one can take it away from you. That is the medicine way and, for you, that is the right way."

"Am I really on that road, Agnes?"

"Yes, but you don't know it yet. You still may not survive."

I felt a sudden attack of anxiety. "Red Dog wants to kill me, doesn't he?"

Agnes smiled. "If he only wished to kill you, you could consider yourself lucky. No, he wants to test you, and what's in store for you could make death look like a picnic. When a shaman puts you to the test, hang on to anything you can. There are four places he can battle you: in fire, wind, earth, or water. If he chases you to some other spot, then you'll know you've lost. Get the hell out of there and give up your dreams. Go back home and collect native Kewpie dolls and forget it. But chances are you'll be caught in the far-away. You won't be able to go anywhere."

I mulled over Agnes' words. I thought about my dream and my passion for Red Dog, about July and her emptiness. It all fit together, and I began to realize how wickedly Red Dog had tricked me. An anger was growing in my belly.

"How dare Red Dog try to manipulate me!" I blurted out the words so unexpectedly that Agnes started to laugh.

"Well, it's about time," she said. "You're beginning to understand, but you're still in love with him. Your eyes tell me. Now that you're getting some sense, I may be able to doctor you. There's one way I know to prevent him from hawking you."

"What can I do?"

"You must go sit at the pool where I first told you of him. Sit there as many days as it takes. Watch and see what happens. Your sister will soon come and heal you."

"You mean sleep out there all alone?"

"Yes, there's no other way for you right now. There will be protection around you. Also, you will have your earring on. Watch out and you'll be okay."

"Who's my sister? What do you mean?"

"She will meet you there."

"You know I don't have a sister, so you must mean something else."

"You must discover that for yourself."

By this time she had gathered food and tied it into a bundle. She seemed to be rushing.

"Do I really have to do this?"

"You do." Agnes was emphatic. She added, "Red Dog will not show himself out there. His honor is on the line, and he will respect your seclusion."

I doggedly rolled up my sleeping bag, not daring to think about the coming night. I looked at Agnes forlornly.

"Go. And don't come back until you have something to tell me."

I nodded and left. I walked away from the cabin like a banished stray, down the trail toward Ruby's. The sky was the blue of a calm and distant sea. I was so weary of being terrified that I just told myself forcibly, "If I die, I die."

That helped somewhat—my mood improved and my steps were softer. All my life was honed to prevent my death.

I stopped to rest several times, and I ate once. I moved at a slackened pace, in tune with the grass and trees and sky. I hiked up hillsides twice for the overview, and once I took a nap, using my bedroll as a pillow. The weather was changing, becoming warmer as the shadows lengthened. By the time I reached the pool, the afternoon light was a golden glaze on the surrounding hills.

I placed my food bundle and sleeping bag on a rock and scanned the area for my spot. A hollow of ground finally attracted me. It was flat, situated in the open above the pond, and sheltered from the wind by a strand of trees. I was far enough away from the pond so that if the animals came down to the water, they wouldn't be disturbed.

I sat by the edge of the water on a flat rock. My dinner was jerky and fried bread. I splashed some water on my face afterward, and collected dead twigs, slightly damp and smelling of earth. Soon, I had a small fire started.

The last faint rays of the sun died, and darkness settled quickly. I crawled into my sleeping bag and put my sneakers under my head. I was surprisingly comfortable. Looking at the full moon, I was lulled by the sound of frogs and crickets across the night distances. I asked the moon never to stop shining, and I felt her light touching some light within me. The last thing I remember, my mind was wandering through some enormous moon-shadowed land.

I awoke the next morning in the same position I had been in when I fell asleep. I was well rested. It was sunrise. I lay there and watched the lights play across the early sky. A gust of brisk wind crossed my face. I dozed a little longer before getting up.

The difference in temperature between shady and sunny was pronounced. I chose to sit on the same flat rock and watch the pool. It was a place where the sun warmed and relaxed me. Agnes had given me strict instructions to sit as still as possible, facing north, to contemplate the water and let it teach me. She said that it was especially important that I exercise self-discipline.

At first, I was distracted by the wind blowing in the high bushes, by the leaves rustling, and by the myriad of insects. I was sitting still with one finger trailing in the water, my only companion a dragonfly that skipped over the pool from time to time. The water rippled with a breeze. I retrieved a leaf that floated by, dripped it up out of the water and let it slip back away. If I were Narcissus, I knew I would have to die.

A hopelessness settled over me when I thought of Red Dog. I was still completely enamored, though I knew it was a horrible trick. The great katchina—I cannot describe the ecstasy the thought gave me. A bird flew in front of me, then another going in the opposite direction. Still another swung around the corner of a tree, moving very fast and low above the water. Some creature off in the wilderness called to his mate.

The sun climbing higher in the sky felt much hotter than usual. I was not myself any longer. I was a dreamer of the flute katchina—considering only him.

Time, eons of time, passed in every moment. I was struggling to see more clearly. I lay down flat on the warm rock and extended my consciousness into the water as if I were slowly turning beneath the tides. Like a fish beneath the surface of the ocean, I was lulled into slumber. I rolled back and forth under the sun, quietly resting on the crest of the sea, unable to change my course or instincts.

I wandered effortlessly through submerged caverns, nudging the lifeless forms silhouetted against the ancient rocks as if begging for a sign. I examined my reflection in underground pools for the clue to being alive that was always lost when I came back to shore. I grasped at the water and at the face of the Kokopelli, only to have my fingers washed clean of any evidence. I was a creature beyond love or hope. I went back into the caverns beneath the surface alone, crying out to the resemblance of a distant god. I recalled my ancient souls and the turnings and torture that had brought me here. I questioned the very soul of the sea within me. It was the beginning, the wisdom of all ages, serenity and truth there in the tide. The water slipped through my fingers, ripples were born and died, bubbles and foam floated away. In the green water, there was quietness. The surface became sky and cloud, and I was left alone at the edge of the shore.

Suddenly, I caught sight of something out of the corner of my eye. I turned slowly and stared straight into the unblinking eyes of a rattlesnake. He was about six feet away from me, his head lifted above his coils, holding me in his quiet gaze. We looked at each other, and then he lowered his head tranquilly, stretched out straight, and went to sleep in the sun, ignoring me.

I watched for any movement, but the snake was still. I couldn't stop looking at him. Then an extraordinary thing happened. A dragonfly that had been flitting around the pool for hours suddenly landed right on the rattlesnake's head. The snake's forked tongue darted out his mouth, and the dragonfly lifted up, hovered over the snake briefly, and flew right at me. The swift motion made me flinch, but it landed on my forehead right between my eyes, stayed there for just an instant, and flew off downstream.

I knew that the dragonfly was the sister I had waited for.

I carefully got up and walked away. I left tobacco for the snake and the dragonfly, hastily collected my things, flung the bundle over my back, and headed off up the trail. When I turned back to look, the snake was still sleeping by the water.

The pale sunlight had turned golden with afternoon. As I walked, I realized that my desire for Red Dog had vanished. Tears of gratitude ran down my cheeks, and I started to run for the cabin. I couldn't wait to tell Agnes.

When I came in sight of the cabin, I let out a wolf howl. Agnes came out on the porch and stood there, grinning from ear to ear. I leapt at her, and we gave each other a big bear hug and went inside. I collapsed into the chair and drank a cup of water.

Agnes asked me what happened, and I explained the events at the pool.

"Please tell me what it means," I asked excitedly. "I can't believe the difference in my perception. What a nightmare this has been!" And I added, "I'm going to get Red Dog!"

Agnes laughed at me. "Yes," she said. "That medicine dragonfly is your sister. She is the guardian and protector of Quetzalcoatl. All creatures that hibernate, such as the bear and the snake, are dreamers. They sleep a long time and they dream. Your sister dragonfly saw your distress and brought you the power from a dreamer to your vision eye. She pulled that obsession from you. It's that simple."

"Your explanation doesn't seem simple to me. But my mind's my own, at least for the time being."

"I'll bet you would love some tea," Agnes said.

I nodded my head. We talked and laughed a while. Then, working together, we prepared dinner. It was a comfort to be back home.

All true sorcerers know how to steal power.

—Agnes Whistling Elk

My happiness was short-lived. I awoke before dawn to fleeting images of my death at the hands of Red Dog.

"Agnes," I whispered. "Agnes."

She didn't answer. It was the first time I had awakened before her. A dismal gray light began to throw slate shadows on the plank floor, and a frayed mist obscured the trees outside. The air was dead still. My sleeping bag was damp and my body felt wrapped in pads of insulation. I was despondent. I knew I would never manage to learn anything. I would never steal the marriage basket. And how could I ever be happy again in my old life? My perspective had totally changed, and yet this medicine world was beyond my reach. This world was too violent and I would never be able to learn all that Agnes wanted me to. I started to sob into my pillow.

"What's Poor Cow crying about so early in the morning?" Agnes asked, turning onto her side and leaning on one elbow.

"Agnes, I'll never be able to steal the marriage basket from Red Dog," I blubbered. "I've wasted my time. He'll destroy me."

"What else is the matter?"

"I'm so stupid."

"Anything else?"

"I can't imagine how I got into this mess in the first place. I can't believe it."

Agnes got out of bed and opened the window to let in the fog. She began heating some water.

"Lynn, stop indulging yourself and listen to me. You have a lot to learn today. We don't have much time, so pay close attention. You need not talk anymore, Poor Cow. You die to your memories. You drink of the water where the great sleeping lynx cat prowls in the moonlight. You forget that someone gave you power. Then the water babies will come along and ask you, 'Where did you get those powers to illuminate?' "

I dried my tears and pulled my blanket around my shoulders. "Agnes, I can't understand you half the time. What are you talking about now? Why are you calling me Poor Cow all of a sudden?"

Sniveling, I watched the fog curling through the open window. Agnes sat down and looked at me intently, then slowly swung her arm and opened her fingers as if she was going to throw something in my face. "This is called throwing sand in the eyes of the buffalo before you kill it, Poor Cow. You don't want the buffalo to see the giveaway."

"What do you mean, and why did you call me Poor Cow again?"

"Because you don't understand the giveaway."

"Who was Poor Cow?"

"Poor Cow was a man. It's not important that he was a man. He could have been a woman. He's you this morning. He went around the village all the time and felt sorry. 'Oh, Dark Sparrow doesn't have any moccasins.' 'Oh, poor Young Bull, he doesn't have a warm blanket.' 'Oh, poor Yellow Eyes, he has a lame leg.' 'Oh, poor me, I'm so unhappy.'

"Poor Cow ran into Twin Coyotes, the medicine man. He was still going around saying, 'Poor everyone.' Everywhere he looked, Poor Cow saw something sad. Twin Coyotes said, 'Hey, Poor Cow, where's your shadow?' Poor Cow looked at his feet and there was no shadow on the ground. It wasn't there. Poor Cow had lost his shadow. 'I don't have one,' he said. 'Don't you think you ought to go find it?' Twin Coyotes asked. 'Yes,' Poor Cow said. 'I don't want to go around without a shadow. I want to find it.'

"Poor Cow went through the village looking for his lost shadow. He looked in all the lodges, feeling sorry for himself. He couldn't find it anywhere. Twin Coyotes saw him one day and said, 'Hey, Poor Cow, did you find your shadow?' Poor Cow said, 'No, I couldn't find it. I give up.' 'Did you try the Sweat Lodge?' Twin Coyotes asked. 'Maybe you took a sweat and left it in there.' 'I'll go look,' Poor Cow said. Poor Cow ran off to the Sweat Lodge. He went inside and found his shadow. In the end, the crier went around the village. 'Good news. Poor Cow found his shadow in the Sweat Lodge,' the crier said. 'Poor Cow is dead.'

"I told you that story because you're like Poor Cow. You see so many things that are unimportant. The things that are very important you are unaware of."

"You're right," I said. "I am a Poor Cow, aren't I? I often feel sorry for myself and the whole world."

My depression was lifting. I got up and ate a piece of bacon and some nuts. Then I sipped my tea and thought for a while.

Agnes finally said, "You've learned about your enemy and you've learned about your opponent. The forces in Beverly Hills are the same as the forces at the water hole that day. In your world, they call them insanity and death."

"Aren't opponents and enemies the same?" I asked.

"Well, you have a lot of enemies around you—cancer, disease—the things that you have to fend off, like evil people bent on destruction. But it's a very great thing to have an opponent."

"What do you mean?"

"Say you were a writer and you decided to pick Anaïs Nin, that lady you once talked with, as your worthy opponent. You tried to beat her in creativity and ideas. In a sense, you would use her to see yourself. You don't want her to fail—you would lose your model. What does a medicine person want you to do? They want to give away to you until you have power so that you can become a worthy opponent to another worthy warrior."

I asked, "How does competition relate to opposition?"

"I just told you the world is pretty much the same everywhere. Competition is the ugly sister of opposition. In true opposition, there's nothing to gain or lose. You can only benefit. If you start to think that you and the opposition are mutually supportive, you can lose a lot. You can't depend on your opponent. You can only depend on yourself. No one is going to save you. A contrary, a heyoka, sees the world as opposition and learns not to separate the inward moon lodge from the outward sun lodge. You can't compete with anything."

"Can you compete with death?"

"No, you can only oppose death. Competition is self-centered, but opposition is ennobling." She paused. Her eyes flashed out at me. "How are you going to compete with the winter?" she asked.

"You can't," I said.

"But you can oppose the winter, for instance, in a worthy way. It gets back to spirits. A guy dreams up a T.V.—everyone competes to make the best, but they never stop to honor the uniqueness of the dream. I can sit here for days trying to give you a metaphor for truth. Trying, forever, to wake you. But you have to be willing to eat and drink the earth, the sun, and the universe to know that all these things are within you."

Agnes wagged her head. My depression was gone. I wanted to lounge around all day, thinking about the things she had told me, but Agnes wouldn't allow it. "Come on," she said. "Put on this sweater. We're going for a walk."

I started to object.

"Get up," Agnes insisted, pulling me onto my feet.

I took the sweater.

"Where are we going?" I asked once we were outside. She motioned with her eyes, and I followed her down the trail toward Dead Man's Creek.

The gray air was cool and invigorating, and the forest was still blanketed with fog. Young saplings were growing under the shade of older trees. Agnes turned sharply off the trail toward a young ash tree, bent it gently, and motioned for me to look.

"Normally this is the kind of child you look for, but we can't do it that way. It takes a week or two to dry."

"What is this tree for?" I asked. "A bow? Or a shield?"

"It's for a pipe to give away. You're going to make it."

I couldn't imagine being able to make a pipe, and I said so.

"Just pay close attention," Agnes said. She sounded impatient.

I followed as she walked rapidly back to the cabin through the mist. Before we entered, she picked up a cut and dried sapling hanging against the side of the cabin. It looked like the one she had just shown me, except that it had been shortened and whittled on. Inside, she laid the piece of wood across the table.

"Sit down," she ordered, very formally.

She rummaged around with her back to me, then turned quickly and threw a hunting knife spinning through the air. It stuck into the table, not a foot away from my hand.

I recoiled.

"You're not paying attention. Whittle off the rest of the bark. Bear down evenly with the blade."

I was afraid to say anything more, and my hand trembled as I pulled out the knife and started carving lightly. The remaining bark came off easily.

"Good. Now carve a little circle at this end, like this." After she cut, she handed me back the knife. "Now go ahead while I heat some water and make tea."

Agnes watched me for about twenty minutes while I worked, giving instructions from time to time. Then she went to a shelf, produced a very beautiful gray pipestone bowl for the pipe, and showed me how it would fit on the stem.

"Now, Lynn," she said, handing me a coathanger. "Take this and straighten it out."

I worked on the hanger for about ten minutes with a pair of pliers and the heel of my tennis shoe until the wire was pretty straight. I showed Agnes my work.

"Heat it up in the stove." she said. "Red hot."

I did as she told me, holding the straightened hanger with a towel. When the wire glowed red, I took it out, wondering what I was supposed to be doing.

"Now hold the stem and push the coathanger down through the center and burn out the pulp. That's right. See, it goes through fairly easily because it's so hot."

The wire did, in fact, hollow the pith without too much trouble.

"Pretty good," Agnes said. "Get rid of the wire, sit down, and start whittling to make the stem flatter."

Agnes was smiling, and we were both pleased. She placed a small handmade bead loom and several jars of different colored beads in front of me. Then came various pieces of leather and thong, and several plumes and feathers.

"When you finish whittling, make whatever design you like with these beads, and bead a couple of inches of the stem. You can choose any feathers or plumes to hang there." She tapped the front of the stem with her finger.

I was delighted with the project and lost myself in it. I decided to make a lightning design in turquoise, yellow, and red, with a border of dark blue beads. I didn't look up until late in the afternoon, when strains of flute music came in through the partially opened window. Moments later, Ruby burst fiercely in through the cabin door.

"July is bad—real bad," she said to Agnes, ignoring me completely.

The music outside the cabin door was very weak.

I got up and out fast. On the porch, July sat back against the wall, looking half dead, just as frightening as Ruby. I scurried back inside—trapped between an old crazy woman and a near-dead young one.

"Can I get her anything?" I asked in alarm.

"Just her spirit—that's all," Ruby snarled at me.

"Now, now, Ruby," Agnes said, placing a hand on her shoulder. "Hissing and spitting isn't going to do any good. Let's go have some fun." She looked at me. "Grab your jacket, Lynn. We're going to go give Red Dog a big kick in the ass. Do everything exactly as I tell you and keep out of the way."

We left July with some food and water, and the three of us took off at a trot up the trail, the two old women running like young girls. It suddenly occurred to me that we were hurrying to some kind of confrontation with Red Dog.

"Oh, my God," I yelled. "Red Dog."

Agnes and Ruby stopped in their tracks ahead of me and I caught up.

"What are we doing?" I asked.

"Silence, idiot," Agnes said. "Do you want everything for a hundred miles to shout it to Red Dog that we're coming?"

"No," I said in a frightened whisper.

Both Agnes and Ruby gave me furious, evil looks. Ruby pinched my arm and said, "Never talk. Know what you're doing and strike." I jerked at the pain in my arm.

We took off running again and didn't stop until we were a hundred or more yards from Red Dog's cabin. Then we slowed to a walk and found cover.

Agnes whispered harshly in my ear, "You and I will hide behind these trees. Blend in with them and don't move a muscle until I tell you to."

We were now about thirty yards away. Agnes signaled something to Ruby with her hand. I watched from behind a tree as Ruby sauntered off down toward the cabin, bent, and picked up a handful of rocks. She hesitated a moment, then started throwing the rocks onto the tin roof. Each one, as it hit, caused a great clattering noise.

Red Dog's head shot out of the doorway.

"Who the hell's making the noise?" he called.

Ruby made no attempt to hide. Instead, she started making hysterical gobbling sounds like a turkey, strutting back and forth in the yard.

Red Dog took a couple of barefooted steps out onto the porch, still disheveled and wearing the same khakis and olive-drab jacket. Ben and Drum peered carefully out of the door behind him. I could see the red hair on Red Dog's chest. I tested my feelings for him. Nothing remained except loathing.

"Ruby, get the hell off my property!" he bellowed. His voice chilled the forest.

Ruby threw another rock. A direct hit on the roof sounded like someone beating on a garbage can.

"You're lucky I don't burn this place down," Ruby yelled, picking up a board and smashing it over the old rusty plow. "You stole my wire cutters, and don't tell me you didn't."

"I did not steal your wire cutters, you old witch," Red Dog yelled back. "Now get the hell out of here!"

"You'll be sorry, you bastard. I'll get the Indian police over here. They'll get my cutters back."

"You just do that and we'll see what happens. I'll tell them what you've been doing."

"You wouldn't dare," Ruby screamed, throwing another rock, this time at his window. It hit the sill and bounced, cracking the glass. "I'll teach you to steal wire cutters that don't belong to you!"

I couldn't believe it. Here were a powerful sorcerer and a medicine woman taking each other to task over wire cutters. It made absolutely no sense.

Ruby lobbed an empty pop bottle. It landed at the foot of the porch, hit a flag rock, and exploded. Glass flew in all directions. Red Dog leapt back, and Ben and Drum completely vanished inside.

Ruby was extraordinary. Though blind, she somehow knew the distance between where she was standing and the dusty rocks that formed the crumbling foundation of Red Dog's porch. The fragments of bottle had settled in a semicircle not quite touching Red Dog's feet. Such accuracy was not coincidence. Ruby was not the least incapacitated by her blindness. She turned her head a little to one side like an old crow cocking its head. Her opaque eyes, never turned directly toward Red Dog, were cold and unblinking in the pale light.

"I know you're up to something, Ruby," Red Dog yelled. He waved his arm. "Just get the hell out of here."

He went back in the cabin and slammed the door.

Now Ruby really started making a racket. She made high, screeching bird calls and cackles, and strutted around like a turkey some more. She threw rock after rock on the tin roof. The door finally burst open, and Red Dog came back out again—furious. His face was red and menacing, his red beard and hair sticking out in all directions. In spite of the fact that I was well hidden I was shaking. Agnes looked like the tree she was hiding behind.

"This is my property, Ruby," Red Dog shrieked. "And you better cut it out!"

Ruby also shrieked. "Ha! What are you doing on the reserve anyway? Why don't you live with other white people? None of the Indians can stand you. You stink, you filthy wasichu."

"It's none of your business where I live," Red Dog hollered. "I can live any damn place I want to."

"Give me my wire cutters!"

"I wouldn't give them to you if I had them."

"I'll burn this goddamn place down!"

"There'll be one dead old lady if you try it!"

Ben and Drum were lurking behind Red Dog, nodding in agreement. Red Dog was seething mad, and so, seemingly, was Ruby.

"Get out of here, Ruby," Red Dog shouted. "Everyone knows you're plumb crazy. They're right."

"Kiss my ass!" Ruby roared.

She stomped around to the side of the cabin and threw the door to Red Dog's toolshed open. Inside, she started clanking around. The men, with Red Dog in the lead, took a few small steps toward her.

"I knew it," she yelled. "I found them."

She strutted back into the yard, brandishing her find.

"Those are my wire cutters," Red Dog said quickly. "I bought them in Brandon last summer on sale. I didn't steal them." He took a pace forward but didn't leave the porch. "Those aren't wire cutters anyway, you stupid old bitch. Those are vise grips. Drum, aren't those vise grips?"

"Yeah," Drum said in a hoarse voice. "They sure are. I remember."

"Show a little respect for me," Ruby yelled. "I'm not that gullible. I don't care what they are. They're mine!"

Red Dog's voice was growling. "What's an old woman like you want with wire cutters anyway?"

"I want to build a big fence around my cabin to keep out tool snatchers like you."

"You give those wirecutters back, or I'll . . . "

"You'll what?"

"I'll take them away from you!"

"It'd be just like you to take something you'd stolen away from an old blind lady."

"Why, you old . . . " Red Dog shouted. He stamped his feet and punched the side of his cabin.

Ruby turned and started walking off toward the road defiantly. She threw out her hips and extended the vise grips high.

"Come on," Red Dog shouted to Ben and Drum. "We can't let her get away with that!" His face was even redder, and his eyes blazed with fire. "Let's get her!"

The three men trampled off down the road chasing Ruby. They were screaming and yelling at the top of their lungs. The cabin door was left ajar.

I turned to Agnes to ask if we should go help Ruby. She was standing there, then gone, and I turned in time to see her enter the cabin. It was as if she had taken a leap of thirty yards and landed soundlessly on the porch. Then she reappeared, seeming to pass through a part of the door. She had a grin on her face, and she was holding a gourd. Then, she seemed to snap forward and was suddenly standing next to me again.

I was so frightened my stomach hurt. I wanted to double over, but before I could do anything, Agnes slapped me.

"That won't help. Be a warrioress," she demanded.

We ran toward Agnes' cabin, faster than I had ever run. Without warning, Ruby was suddenly running beside us. It happened so unexpectedly, I was terrified.

"Did you get it?" Ruby asked Agnes.

"Yes," Agnes said, breathing hard. She touched her with the small, beaded gourd.

The narrow trail rang with their diabolical laughter. As we swung into Agnes' yard, we fell rolling on the ground. I was laughing hysterically.

"You should have seen Red Dog's face when he started chasing you." Agnes pointed at Ruby. "You sly one." She roared again with laughter.

They slapped and patted and congratulated each other. They hopped up and down, fell, and rolled some more.

I stopped laughing abruptly. "Ruby, how did you get away from them?"

"I let them think they had scared me. I dropped the vise grips and ran away."

"But won't Red Dog ransack your cabin?" I asked in alarm.

Ruby and Agnes stared at me.

"No, that would be deceitful," Ruby said thoughtfully. "There's nothing in that for him. I wouldn't ransack his cabin. I'm not that kind of person."

"Yeah, well you did tonight," I said.

"No," Ruby said. "We are merely returning something that belongs to July. A human's spirit is her own."

"Every confrontation with Red Dog is a challenge to his personal power, Lynn," Agnes said.

"I don't know," said Ruby. "But that gets to be boring sometimes."

I was completely confused, but I started laughing again.

We all became conscious of July at the same moment. We turned and looked at her. She was still sitting in the same place, with the plate of food and her water now turned over. She blew air into the flute in shallow puffs. Her eyes were dim.

"We have to give back to her," Agnes said. "Reawaken the reflected painting."

Ruby and Agnes bent over July and led her to the center of the yard. She was docile.

Ruby fussed over July and turned her facing west. The sun was under the horizon, but the last light was still fading. Leading her by the waist, she directed her to stand in a certain spot. Agnes walked right behind July.

The old women were working deliberately, unhurriedly. When everything seemed to be in order, Ruby motioned to Agnes. Agnes lifted the gourd directly over July's hair from behind. Ruby pushed on the girl's stomach, Agnes twisted her hands on the gourd, and I heard a sharp, cracking sound like a pistol shot. A plume of smoke swirled around on the top of July's head and seemed to be sucked down into it by a straight silver thread.

For the second time that evening, I doubled over in pain.

Agnes yelled at me. "Go get me a blanket for July."

I staggered to the cabin and came back with a blanket from Agnes' bed. Ruby put it around July's shoulders.

They each took an arm and made her walk back and forth across the yard, encouraging her in low whispers.

"What just happened?" I asked.

"July walked across," Agnes said simply.

"Don't let that damned Red Dog ever fool you again," Ruby said sternly to July.

July was holding her head in her hands. She wasn't the same person. She sobbed quietly.

Then her eyes cleared and she started to smile. "I couldn't get back. Is there anything to eat?"

"Lynn, get July some deer jerky," Agnes said.

We all walked to the cabin.

"What's this doing here?" July asked, picking up her abandoned flute off the ground.

"Oh, no," Ruby cried. She snatched the flute away from her, cracked it over her knee, and flung the pieces in the air.

July shrugged.

There was a sudden whir of dark wings, and the crow landed on July's shoulder and cawed loudly in her ear.

Agnes turned to me. "Crow has been flying around looking for July's lost spirit. That's her bird. Now they are united again. We should all be happy."

Inside the cabin, July ate ravenously. When she was finished, we were introduced. I sensed that she knew many things I would yet have to learn.

Late in the night, after Ruby and July left, I lay silently in my sleeping bag, wondering what would be next. Nothing made any sense.

All I knew for sure was that I still wanted the marriage basket.

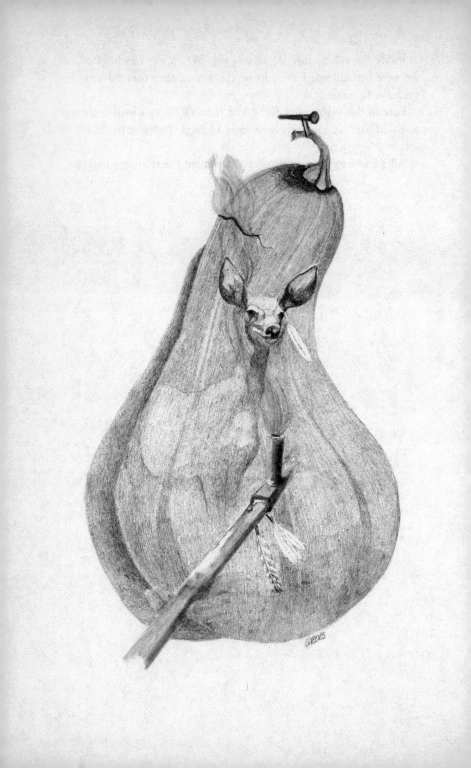

I leave you within the mirror of creativity and touching the world circle.
—Hyemeyohsts Storm

Agnes shook me awake gently. It was pitch black. Even after Agnes had lit the lantern, the window looked as if a black curtain had been drawn across it. Agnes' eyes told me that I was to face some immediate challenge. As I pulled on my jeans, I noticed that my fingers were twitching.

"Red Dog is going to be pretty mad if he catches you prowling around his cabin," she said matter-of-factly.

My stomach quaked. "I'm sure that's true."

"He will want revenge now. You must be very careful. He has a million tricks. You saw what he did to July—she very nearly didn't survive. You must not do anything or make any decision without first holding counsel with me. You can continue to watch for a chance, but don't go after the basket. Do you understand?"

"You mean I shouldn't make a move toward the cabin without asking you first?"

"That's right. You cannot afford another mistake."

"Do you still want me to go there and watch for an opportunity?"

"Yes, but if Red Dog sets the marriage basket in front of your nose, come back and ask me before you try to take it."

"Why do I even have to go if I'm powerless to get it?"

"Going there and watching is a test of your ability and will as a warrioress. Don't let them find your hiding place. This contest has become very serious. It's a matter of life and death."

I took a deep breath and sat down to a meager breakfast, forcing myself to eat. I reflected over the many days I had spied on the cabin in order to steal the basket. My goal seemed to be getting further from my reach.

"Why are you sending me out so early?"

"Red Dog is a sound sleeper and a late riser, and maybe this time he won't feel your presence. He's so damned unpredictable, it's the only thing I can think of."

It was the first time I had heard Agnes sound unsure of herself. She threw her chair back, got up and paced back and forth slowly. "I hope I'm telling you the right thing, Lynn. I just don't know now what you should do. One thing's for sure, if they get you cornered, grab hold of your earring and run for your life. Are you sure you still want that crazy basket?"

"Agnes, what kind of question is that? Of course I want the basket."

"Maybe I'm getting senile, Lynn." She shook her head. "It would be a whole lot easier for me if you'd just get the hell back to Beverly Hills."

"Agnes! What's the matter with you?"

"Just go get that basket and don't come back until you do."

"Agnes, you just told me not to do anything without asking you first."

"Well, if that's what I told you, that's what you'd better do."

I felt a strange tingle go through me. "Please don't confuse me, Agnes. Please!"

She answered in Cree.

"Agnes, I don't know what you're saying. Please don't do this." I was starting to completely panic.

Agnes didn't answer. She started signing to me—using sign language! I ran to her and shook her—she seemed limp.

"Lynn! Lynn!" Agnes said loudly. "Red Dog is attacking me. Do what I told you to do first. Come back. I hope I'm alive when you get here."

"Can I do anything for you?" I shouted.

"Yes, you can go. Now. Don't get murdered."

I pulled on a brown sweater and grabbed a few pieces of jerky. I crammed the meat in both pockets.

Agnes hugged me at the door. "I am full, Little Wolf. Be careful of the dogs."

Agnes had obviously mistaken me for her child of long ago. She suddenly screamed, clutching her throat, and fell to the floor kicking. "Get that damned bull!" she screamed. "Get him good!"

I started screaming myself.

Agnes sprang to her feet. "Awake now, honey?" she asked in a sarcastic but lucid voice.

"Yes," I stammered, my throat sore from screaming.

"You'll go for any old act, won't you, Lynn? I was testing to see if you can be trusted to act independently. You can't."

"You mean that was all an act, a joke?" I didn't know if I was relieved or mad.

"Not a joke—a test. You're not ready yet."

"I don't think that was very fair."

"Oh, you don't, Poor Cow. Well, neither will Red Dog when he kicks the hell out of you. He won't think it's fair that you're so lame." Agnes looked me up and down. "I also tricked you to give a blow to your solidity. You may never get but this one chance at stealing the basket, and I want you to be successful. So come back swiftly and tell me anything you think is important for me to know."

"Okay," I said.

I looked at Agnes for a moment, then I was out of the door. There were no stars in the black morning sky, but my feet knew where to run, and how to be silent. The only sound was the distant hooting of an owl.

I started crawling in the thick underbrush about a hundred yards from Red Dog's cabin, then concealed myself forty or so yards away. As the first slivers of light broke on the horizon, I lay flat and still, watching and waiting. At about nine, Drum came out yawning with a tin cup of coffee in his hand. He sat down on the steps and sipped his coffee.

"Damned troublemaker," he cursed.

I smiled, thinking about Ruby pelting the place with rocks.

Drum turned around and called, "Get up, Ben. It's time to go to work."

I heard Ben answer, but the sound was too garbled to understand. When Ben came outside, he was carrying a cup of coffee and the coffee pot. They yawned and wisecracked, stretched and scratched.

They went inside and were gone over an hour, then came back outside again, wearing tattered work overalls instead of their usual jeans. They lugged an enormous roll of chicken wire from the shed to the front porch, then went back for hammers, saws, bars, cutters, trays of nails, chains, clips, and other things I couldn't recognize. It was a queer array of junk scattered about the porch, and Ben and Drum stood looking at it as if it were a complex problem in logic.

"That damned old woman!" Drum shouted, picking up a heavy hammer and throwing it back down. "We wouldn't have to do all this work if it weren't for her."

"Yeah," Ben said in his usual monosyllabic manner.

"Do you want to roll and I'll cut or do you want to cut, and I'll roll?"

Ben scratched his head. "I don't care as long as it gets done."

"I'll tell you what," Drum said. "I'll stand on the edge of the wire and you roll and cut."

"Don't you think we should measure first?" Ben asked.

Now it was Drum's turn to scratch his head. "Oh yeah, I didn't think of that."

There was an argument over who would hold what end of the tape measure. Drum lost.

"Thirty-nine—make it forty-two to be on the safe side. Forty-two inches," Drum said, holding the tape to the window frame.

"I can't remember that," Ben said.

"Well, go find a damned pencil!"

"All right. You don't have to yell."

After a few minutes, Ben came back with paper and pencil. "Now what did you say it was, Drum?"

The measuring of the cabin windows took forever. Ben had to get a stool for the side window and a step ladder for the back one.

They complained every few minutes about Ruby. The cursing and bickering were constant, and the smallest task seemed to require a debate. But invariably they settled on the most ridiculous manner to proceed.

"Damn her!" Ben cursed, as he unrolled the old rusty chicken wire. Drum held the end down by standing on it.

Each time Ben let go of the roll in order to cut a piece of wire with long-handled tin snips the roll snapped back inward, scratching or cutting his hand. "Ouch, goddamn it! That lousy old bitch!"

"Gimme those," Drum said, grabbing the snips. "God, are you ever dumb. Let me do it."

He took a step too many forward, forgetting he was standing on the buckling wire to hold it down. The wire flipped up and tore his overalls.

"Goddamn that wire!" he yelled. His voice echoed through the trees. He fingered the torn pants leg. "Look at what that old hag did."

It took them hours to get the unevenly cut pieces of chicken wire to fit over the windows. It was like an enormous geometric puzzle. Then Red Dog came out.

"You jackasses! What's taking you so long?" he roared. Ben and Drum shrank back from his glare. "Get that stuff nailed up there right now and be quick about it. Move, goddamn it!"

Ben and Drum grabbed oversized hammers and started pounding nails at random. Watching, Red Dog shook his head in disgust. "Billions of people, and I get stuck with you two nincompoops as apprentices."

Ben and Drum hammered faster.

"I want those locks on the toolshed door by nightfall," Red Dog bellowed. "You two better have it done, too."

They hammered wildly now.

"You can't trust anyone these days," Red Dog said, scowling.

"I'll get even with them. I'm going to make their white girl pay for this."

He went back in and slammed the door,

Remembering the photograph of the marriage basket I had seen so long ago, I stared at the cabin, and tried to imagine it in there. Agnes had somehow reinforced my need for it, and I would rather die than leave it behind.

"Ohhh!" Drum winced. He dropped his hammer and held his thumb between his legs, yowling in pain. "Can't you do anything, Ben?"

The crooked chicken wire buckled forward and fell to the ground from the window where he had been nailing.

I knew that all three of those men were alchemists of the highest order, but on the physical plane, at least, they were absurdly inefficient. Ben and Drum seemed to defeat their own efforts at every turn. It was an endless meandering comedy of incompetence, like a bad movie.

Red Dog came out at various times, flailing his arms and cursing. When he stood over them, Ben and Drum made especially farcical blunders. Ben dropped a crowbar on his foot, and Drum pounded with such force he shattered the glass. They seemed to be struggling to see who could be the most idiotic.

Red Dog eventually gave up in disgust and left Ben and Drum to their own devices. By late in the afternoon, they had done all the windows. Then they nailed big metal strips onto the toolshed door and attached a hasp and lock. As Drum stood back to admire the handiwork, Ben dragged out a huge iron lever. It clanked to the ground.

"What in hell are you going to do with that?" Drum asked.

"What do you think? I'm fixing a lock on the outhouse. It wouldn't surprise me any if Ruby slipped a rattlesnake in the hole."

"I don't think even Ruby would do that, Ben."

"I don't care. I'm putting it up anyway."

"Well, she'll never get in the toolshed again, not unless she uses a stick of dynamite."

"Yeah. Well, she's not going to get in the crapper either." Ben dragged the wedge of old rusted iron across the yard. "Aren't you going to help me?" he called to Drum. "It's not as if you don't have to use it too."

Drum helped. It was very late when the locks were in place and the tools were put away.   \

"Look at these windows," Drum said.

"Boy, the outhouse is better than a pay toilet," Ben said.

"I think we did a good job, don't you?"

"I sure do. We ought to hire out on construction. Hell, I bet we could be engineers if we wanted to."

Red Dog walked up and joined them. "You two couldn't engineer a bird feeder."

Ben and Drum were crestfallen. Red Dog shook his head sadly.

I was giggling in spite of myself. The whole thing was like a Keystone Cop routine.

"We did the best we could, Red Dog," Ben said in a hurt voice.

"What do you expect?" Drum said. "Neither one of us are carpenters, are we?"

They were all in the cabin before I could hear Red Dog's answer. I tried to relax my nerves a little bit. Nothing happened for a while, then Red Dog, Ben, and Drum burst out the cabin door, slammed it, and whooped and hollered into the twilight. Their arms around each other and singing, they stumbled off down the road. I lay there watching them walk out of sight. I reasoned that they were going into Crowley to carouse. I was sure they were drunk.

I didn't dare try to take the basket without first consulting Agnes—not after the experience of this morning. I ran as fast as I could to her cabin and flew in through the door, so out of breath I couldn't talk. Agnes scanned me in a glance from her chair.

"Agnes," I said excitedly. "I think they're gone. They all went stumbling and singing off toward town. They're drunk."

"They must be," Agnes said, getting up. "Now's your chance.

Be careful you're not being tricked. Keep courage, Lynn, and remember everything I've taught you. Go quickly and steal the basket."

I left in a hurry. It was dark, with a soft sliver of moon in the clear sky. About forty yards away from Red Dog's cabin, I stopped. There was no sign of life anywhere, and the cabin was dark. I was shivering. I moved closer, knelt down behind some brush, and felt the cold damp earth with my hands. Then I moved closer and crouched down behind the silhouette of a tree stump.

"Hello, dear," Drum suddenly said.

My blood ran cold. I realized I was holding onto his leg. He had bent his body into the shape of a naked tree—bent over, his arms hanging out grotesquely. In the darkness, I could not distinguish his form from that of the scrub trees nearby. I let loose of his leg and backed off, terrified.

Another shadowy figure was standing to my immediate right, still another behind me. They had me surrounded.

"Lady, get your ass out of here or I'll nail it to my wall!"

It was Red Dog. The three dark forms all stole toward me at once, and I gave a scream and fled, hearing Red Dog's bellowing laughter as I ran. My foot hit a stump, I went down head over heels, got up again, and ran down the path toward Agnes' cabin.

"Get her!" someone shouted. "Over there!"

Ben and Drum began hurling large rocks at me as I ran. The stones were coming close. Any one of them could have crushed my skull. They were still laughing.

I ran and ran over the rocky path to Agnes' house, only realizing I was out of danger when I collapsed at her door. "I was tricked," I yelled. "They nearly killed me."

Agnes laughed at me. "They wouldn't bother killing you because your attempt was so amusing."

I wanted to cry. "It wasn't very amusing to me."

Agnes' eyes thrust out at me impishly.

"I knew that Red Dog was tricking you," Agnes said.

"You knew it and you sent me there anyway?"

"Yes, I wanted to see the fireworks. As soon as you told me they were all drunk, I knew what they were up to. Sorcerers are never

drunk unless it's a form of deception. I had to show them how
weak you were to fool them. You tricked them by falling into their
trap. They have no respect for you—none. It's good. They will feel
no urgency to shield themselves from you." She poured me a cup
of warm tea and pushed it in my direction. "Sit down," she said.
"Nothing is going to happen to you right this moment. Drink it.
Enjoy some tea."

I sipped a few swallows.

"You see, Lynn, those guys think you're a foolish, stupid woman
and pose no threat to anyone. They think you will be ashamed of
yourself and go away. As long as they think that, they are
vulnerable. This is the best time. Many humans fail their vision,
but I hope you are tough. You must be a huntress, a warrioress.
You must teach us all what it is to have a dream. Go back and
watch through the night. Your passion for the marriage basket is
irrevocable. You have come here into this world to discover your
way. You've found it and now you must take it."

Agnes got up from the table and went to the dresser. In a few
moments, she was back with her medicine bundle and my
buckskin dress and moccasins.

"Put these on," she said. "Don't dishonor them. They are full of
woman's energy."

I quickly undressed. The air chilled my skin, but when I put the
buckskins on I was instantly warm. The beautiful clothing felt like
a caressing skin.

Agnes picked up her medicine bundle. "Outside," she pointed.
"Bring the blanket."

I grabbed the blanket and followed her into the yard. She told
me to spread the blanket out on the ground and smooth it.

"Sit there," she said sternly.

We sat down at opposite ends of the blanket. Between us, Agnes
untied the rattles that hung from the bundle and unrolled the
hide, exposing the contents. She sorted and laid everything
out—several black, yellow, and red ribbons, dried flowers, quartz
crystals, pieces of hair or possibly scalps, an owl claw, several
beaded medicine bags tied at the top, and some things I didn't
recognize.

Agnes leaned forward and braided two owl feathers in my hair.

"Do any of these things speak to you?" she asked, motioning down at the articles.

"I don't know."

I felt a sudden force from something that looked like a gnarled rock. "That," I pointed.

Agnes nodded approvingly. "That is a grandfather. He is over ninety years old—a grandfather peyote button. I often feel his power myself."

As my eyes went over the bundle I noticed, alongside some feathers, a torn half of a twenty dollar bill.

"Where did you get that?" I exclaimed, choking.

I thought back to Guatemala and the young Indian man who had torn my money in half. I still carried my piece.

"It is broken money from the south and spoke of your coming."

The color drained from my face.

Agnes picked up a small pipe and handed it to me. I held the delicate stem in my hand. She placed four eagle feathers in a circle with the quills facing inward, almost touching.

"Each feather represents one of the directions," she said. "This is a sign that you are in the center of the lodge."

I handed her back the pipe. She tamped a coarse yellow tobacco she took from one of the beaded leather bags into the pipe bowl, lit it, and took several puffs.

"I want you to have plenty of this friend-smoke," she said, handing it to me. "Suck deeply and rub your stomach."

The pipe was warm and smooth, like new bone. The bittersweet smoke made me heady.

"We can hold up this pipe together. The grandparents are with you in the realization of your dream. This friend-smoke is a guest from the weeping tipi of the old woman who talks to roses."

Agnes' face seemed to stand out while she was speaking. Her voice was soothing. I could feel pressure on my ears like compressed air and it seemed important that I tell Agnes that I respected and loved her.

I found that I could actually eat the smoke as if it were some thin cotton substance. Agnes could have been a girl of eighteen, with long braids down her back. I tried to speak of my inner realization, but everything, every thought, seemed to collapse inward. I had been sitting on the blanket forever and this moment would never cease to be.

Agnes took the glowing pipe from me. "This medicine pipe has been smoked for a thousand years, and this sweet herb is a secret herb. Its spirit is woman. It is a giveaway to the warrioress within you to make you strong in battle."

Agnes stood up and motioned for me to do the same. My body seemed to rise up by an unfamiliar will of its own.

"The white lady of the north who lives in the forest and controls all the animals is listening to us. But there are also medicine deceivers wanting to steal the power of this many-forked heyoka place from you. With this friend-smoke, you will see them. They make long, pointed arrows against your sisters. They feed off your dreams without regard for your hunger. Their pouch holds bad medicine and their heart is evil."

Agnes stomped on the ground in front of her. "Do it," she said. I stomped also.

"My daughter," Agnes said. "My crafty wolf. Now is the time that you look to the southeast, the place of the great peace chiefs. Women stood there first. Now woman must stand there again and balance the camp. This pipe must be held evenly over the earth. My heart will be full if you succeed."

She took some sort of meal from a leather bag and sprinkled it over me. She reached into her shirt, and brought forth a knife inside a white doeskin sheath from between her breasts. She unsheathed it. It had a chipped flint blade. She held up her hand and pressed the point into her thumb.

Blood rolled down the palm of her hand and off her wrist, dripping onto the blanket. She drew her pierced thumb across the top of my head, next to the hairline. I felt a wetness. She kept her hand held up, like a welcoming salute.

"The blood painting your forehead is the blood of a medicine woman. It is good blood from the sweet river of my body. My blood binds it for all women. I am heyoka hand and I say so. Your red road has the heart of us all. I am pleased I can mark your way."

She handed me the sheath and knife, which now appeared to be bone or ivory instead of chipped flint. It looked extremely sharp.

"Put this on your belt. This knife is sacred, brought back from the faraway. If you can get to the basket, this is the only knife that can cut the fibers. You will know what I mean if you manage to get to the marriage basket."

I resheathed it and attached it to my belt.

"You sit here now," Agnes said, "on this blanket. Be silent and still. In the deep of this night, I have felt the presence of the great white lady of the north. If you are chosen to do this thing, she will send an animal down to talk to you. Do not be afraid—she may send a deer or a badger, or even a skunk. You can stay here until sunup. If nothing happens, go anyway. But if an animal comes around you, consider yourself doubly fortunate. The eternal prophetess has made you as sacred as herself."

Agnes rolled up her bundle and retied it. When I realized she was about to go, my deepest fears returned.

"But Agnes," I said, "those three never leave the property."

She looked up. "Lynn, you're going to have to get by them somehow. You'll have to figure out how. Don't think about it or your power will dry up. You are full and I can see it."

I didn't feel very full. I wondered if the friend-smoke had robbed me of my bravery.

"Agnes," I begged.

"I've done all I can do for you now. Linger here awhile. Friend-smoke told me the northern lady who glows in blue light is deciding if she should send a lover to comfort you." She shrugged. "But it's up to her. Remember, if you use the knife, cut quickly."

Agnes turned and left me sitting on the blanket. The night was heavy and dark, and I closed my eyes. Behind me, I heard the brush rustle. Something was snarling, not far away. I heard soft footsteps off to my left—some large creature. I heard panting, then smelled a strange musky odor. I wanted to jerk around and look. Then the beast actually pressed his muzzle into my hair. To my horror, he licked my neck. It was a whiskered animal, its tongue was rough.

I opened my eyes and stared at the face of a lynx. He was panting, mouth open. He stretched out and started to purr, and I began to stroke him. His great long body rippled with muscles. With two paws he hopped up on my shoulders so that I was looking directly into his green eyes, jumped down, and ran around me playfully in a circle. He reversed directions, circled the other way, paused, cocking his head as cats do, and growled.

"You're beautiful," I said. The lynx was the animal Agnes had told me about.

The cat circled around me, then stood directly in front of me, perhaps fifteen yards away. He came at me, pawing the air, and sprang directly over me. I turned in time to see him bounding away with long, clean jumps, disappearing into the dense brush.

Near Red Dog's cabin, I crawled through the underbrush, came to a vantage point, and lay out flat on the ground. I covered myself with dirt and leaves, and watched and waited.

Dawn cracked, and birds began to chirp. Insects began hopping and winging, and small ants crawled over my hand. Butterflies danced in the yard. Something was about to happen—for better or for worse. All my instincts were primed for struggle.

I heard voices from the cabin that I couldn't distinguish. My perceptions seemed heightened. Then Red Dog came out on the cabin porch. I noticed that the birds stopped chirping.

"Drum, come out here," Red Dog called.

A moment later, the door opened. Drum was holding his coffee cup.

"Yeah?" Drum inquired.

"Get me my digging stick. Don't get it confused with my walking stick. I'm going to go get a batch of wild turnips for dinner tonight."

Drum went inside and returned with the stick. Red Dog took it and headed west up into the hills, disappearing into the tree line. Drum sat down on the steps to drink his coffee. Ben threw open the door and made his usual run for the outhouse.

"What's your hurry, Ben?"

"Got to go," he said, unlocking the newly installed lock. He entered and shut the door.

Some garbled words were exchanged.

Drum walked around to the toolshed.

"Hurry up," he called over his shoulder. "I need to use it."

Drum unlocked the shed latch and went inside. I heard him cursing about Ruby and banging around. A long-handled ax landed on the ground outside. A chain followed. Drum kept knocking things around, obviously trying to find something.

This was it!

I leapt up and headed for the shed, my movements sure and swift. I knew exactly what I was going to do. I shut the shed door and secured the lock in an instant, imprisoning Drum in there with his tools, grabbed the ax and chain, and headed for the outhouse twenty-five yards away.

"Hey," Drum shouted, banging on the shed door. "Hey, what's up? Let me out of here!"

I felt as if I were moving in slow motion. I knew I could never get that complicated thing on the door locked, so I quickly wound the chain around the entire privy, tied it in a knot, and used the ax handle to lever the chain.

Now Ben started pounding from within the outhouse. "You'll get your turn! What are you doing?"

Both Ben and Drum were yelling and cursing and banging on the walls, their tones more and more hostile.

I jerked the knife from its sheath and ran for the cabin. The door was unlocked. It took me a moment to adjust to the darkness inside before I saw it. The basket, the exquisite marriage basket, was sitting on the table in the corner of the cabin. I reached out to take it.

Suddenly, I heard Red Dog's voice. I forced myself to steady the trembling knife as the door flew open. Agnes stood there! Was I hallucinating?

"Agnes, what are you doing here? You're ruining everything."

"Give me the knife," she demanded. "That's the wrong basket—the power basket is hidden. Red Dog has coyoteed you again." She took a step toward me.

"Hold it, Agnes!" I screamed hysterically. I held the knife pointed at her. "Stop right there." My arms shook in uncontrollable spasms.

I had always done anything Agnes wanted me to do, but something was terribly wrong. I was repelled by her. It was as if the whole universe had turned against me. I knew, though, that nothing could stop me. Not even Agnes.

"Look at me, Agnes."

Agnes slowly turned her eyes on mine. They were ruthless and desperate, and I knew they belonged to Red Dog. I must have moaned in fear.

Now the mackinaw and skirt hung on him like discarded clothing on a scarecrow, and luminous fibers shot out from all sides of the marriage basket toward him. Red Dog was connected to the basket by glowing strings of light. There seemed to be ripples coming off his body, and he was turning into something that looked like stacks of bailing wire. The face of a red-headed man with a tangle of red beard began to emerge slowly out of the mass of wires and the disintegrating image of Agnes. As he screamed at me to move away from the basket, the voice began to lower and become a man's voice.

"You dare come here!" he thundered. He looked like a madman—full of scorn and superiority.

I drew up. I held the basket, fibers and all, to my stomach, and kicked the table over in front of me. Then I began cutting the luminous sinewy threads with a strength I didn't know I possessed.

Red Dog was scanning me, hunched over, his head swaying drunkenly back and forth. He was gathering power. His stance was like an angry bull preparing to charge. I fought for my life with every hack of the blade. I pulled and played the basket back and forth as I cut, rolling it against my body, feeling a hot strength spreading through me.

"You don't even know what you're doing. You're changing the forces of balance if you cut me away. You don't understand." He swayed from side to side, still doing his dance of power. "Don't believe Agnes. She's a liar."

"No, Red Dog," I yelled. "You're the liar." And I kept slicing at the remaining fibers.

Suddenly Red Dog lurched crazily forward, reached his hand into the open stove and brought out a handful of glowing coals. He bellowed a horrible sound, flung the coals at my face, and charged. The debris came at me like glowing baseballs. Some of it struck me, and blood started running from my forehead, blurring my vision. I lost my balance but managed to cut the last fiber—I could feel the tension snap under the blade. Red Dog's great bulk landed on me, and I held the basket to me as we crashed to the floor. Then suddenly, his weight was lifting away, and he was turning into a shimmering form above me. I rolled away and stood up as his light began to dissipate. He seemed to wither into that awesome glow. He was moaning, imprisoned. His skin began to hang, as if it were a net flung over his skeleton. He squirmed and twisted. Red Dog was shriveling up and growing old. I watched with horror, still clutching the basket. Then the eerie light was gone, and all that was left was an ancient white-haired man.

I backed away and ran from the cabin. It was over. Perhaps I was mad, but one thing I knew—I had the basket. I could feel it.

It seemed like a living entity, like a coiled serpent, and then I realized that its warm texture was beginning to move. I looked down at its magnificence and felt it slipping. What was happening? It felt as though a part of the basket were actually being absorbed into my body, into my solar plexus. It didn't seem to be a part of its own form any longer, and yet I still held it in my hands.

I could feel blood trickling down my face and thought perhaps I was delirious from an injury. I kept reaching for the basket and looking to see if I had dropped it. Then I experienced a curious sensation; it was as if I were running above myself. My whole body began to shiver, waves running up and down my spine. I don't know how long I was in that ecstasy, but finally a great light burst in my head and my being was silent. I was no longer afraid.

I don't remember how I got back to the cabin, but there was a smile on Agnes' face when she saw me.

"Give me the knife," she said.

I took it off my belt and handed her the sheath. Agnes placed the knife inside her shirt.

I collapsed, and she grabbed me as I fell. When I came to, lying on the bed, it was dark, and Agnes was rubbing foul-smelling ointment on my belly and my aching head. My stomach was bruised.

The kerosene lamps were burning. Outside, Ruby and July were sitting in the moonlight singing in Cree. Agnes was watching my expression carefully.

"Where's the marriage basket, Agnes? I want to see it."

"It's with your things." Agnes went over to the dresser and held it up for my inspection before gently handing it to me. "Lynn, you are now the keeper of the basket. It belongs to you and all women. The sacred aspect of the basket is now within you—you got what you came for."

I nodded, amazed at my sense of well-being. I can only explain it as the feeling I had when I was pregnant. I felt the presence of life within me.

"You'll be fine in a day or two." Agnes gave me a warm smile. "By the way, I have something else for you, this is a time for celebration, a time of vision."

As I sat up in bed, Agnes took a large beaded pipe bag down from the shelf and gave it to me. It had wolf fur along the top.

Tears fell from my eyes. The pipe was the one I had worked on, completely beaded and assembled.

"You have a pipe now," Agnes said, her eyes shining. "Hold it proudly. It's a woman's pipe, a sacred pipe. The laws of the universe are in this pipe, and you have much to learn. Your learning has just started. Now you can begin to see the world as it really is."

Epilogue

After the experiences narrated in this book, I went back to Beverly Hills. I saw all my old friends and went to the old familiar places, but they seemed mere shadows compared to my recollection of them.

I went through the motions for a few weeks, until I could stand it no longer. Without telling anyone, I flew back to Canada to see Agnes. When I walked into the cabin unannounced, she was sitting on the floor, and I positioned myself directly in front of her. I gave her tobacco—a carton of American cigarettes. She took them without saying anything and set them down beside her on the plank floor.

She seemed to have been expecting me.

"Everything's changed," I tried to explain. "I don't know what to do. I want to come back here to your world. I want you to continue teaching me."

She looked at me attentively. "No," she said. Her voice was very firm. "It is not yet time."

"Agnes, you've told me that everything I've learned is sacred and secret. Is that true?"

"Yes, that is true."

"Can't I tell anybody, discuss it with anybody?"

"No."

"Well, what should I do?"

For a moment Agnes looked at me fiercely. She held her arms stiffly in front of her, parallel to the floor, her two fists clenched. Then she slowly unclenched her hands, keeping them in front of her, the fingers pointing upward.

"Do you know what this means?" she asked.

I shook my head. "Is it sign language?"

"Yes. When you open your fingers this way, it means two things. The fingers symbolize people, and opening them means letting go of something. I am telling you to give the spirit world to your people. Let your message fly. Let the eagle fly."

"What does that mean?"

"You've seen a lot, you know a lot; but that's not enough. I told you there would come a time when you would be forced to choose your death. Now is that time. Go write a book and give away what you have learned. Then you may come back to me."

As I drove down the bumpy road away from Agnes, I kept repeating the lines of a Robinson Jeffers poem:

Eagle & Hawk with their great claws & hooded heads tear life to pieces;
Vulture & Raven wait for death to soften it.
The poet cannot feed on this time of the world
Until he has torn it to pieces,
    and himself also.

More Praise for
Medicine Woman:

"*Medicine Woman* has to do with the meaning of life, the role of women, and the wrestling of power away from the forces of evil that hold it."—*Los Angeles Times*

"*Medicine Woman* is a well-written, powerful, and exciting tale of the author's apprenticeship with a medicine woman. . . . As in the Casteneda books, it weaves teachings of shamanic philosphy into the telling of the story."—*Circle*

"Thought-provoking and absorbing."—*New Woman's Times*

"The revealing story of how women from different cultures view each other and learn from each other."—Stan Steiner, author of *The New Indians*

"Lynn Andrews celebrates the power of female spirituality. . . . Her dramatic retelling of shamanistic wisdom and ancient Indian philosophy is rich in authentic detail."—*The Victoria Advocate*

"A fascinating story full of marvelous symbols."—*Books of the Southwest*

"A powerful and beautiful story."—*The Guardian*, London

"Her story tells and reminds us of ancient wisdoms that we can take with us on our own unique journeys through life no matter what heartfelt path we are on."—*WomanSpirit*

"An exciting and insightful story . . . about the interrelatedness of all things."—*The Lammas Little Review*

"A statement of what is called for and possible in all of us."
—*Sojourner*